SELF

Law Dictionary and Exercise Book

MICHAEL HOWARD

INTRODUCTION TO UK LAW VOCABUARY:

UK LAW DICTIONARY AND LEGAL WRITING EXERCISE BOOK

CONTENTS

A. THE ENGLISH LEGAL SYSTEM

1. PEOPLE IN LAW

To Act for/To Act on Behalf of (phrasal verb): This phrasal verb means to represent. Lawyers often use these two phrases to confirm that they are the legal representatives for their client. For example, lawyers commonly use the phrases "I am acting for Mr Smith in this matter" or "I am acting on behalf of Mr Smith in this matter".
Associated Words: Acted for/on behalf of (past simple), Acted for/on behalf of (3rd form).

To Advise (verb): This verb is used when a lawyer provides help and guidance to their client. Lawyers advise clients on a wide range of legal issues from family law to mergers and acquisitions. Please remember that the verb is spelt "to advise" and the noun is spelt "advice". There is a small difference in pronunciation.
Associated Words: Advised (past simple), Advised (3rd form), Advised (adjective), Advice (noun), Family Law (noun), Mergers and Acquisitions (noun).

Attorney (person): This is the name of a lawyer who has qualified in the USA. The term attorney-at-law is the full name. Other countries, including Japan and South Africa, also use the word attorney to describe their lawyers.

Attorney General (person): The Attorney General is the main legal advisor to the Monarchy and the Government in the UK. The primary role is to advise the King or Queen and the Government on the legal consequences of their actions. The Attorney General also represents the Government in the International Court of Justice and supervises the Crown Prosecution Service in criminal legal proceedings.
Associated Words: Government (noun), Monarchy (noun).

Bar Council (noun): The Bar Council is the professional association of barristers in England and Wales. This association regulates their professional etiquette, activities and the terms and conditions of their membership. The full name of the association is the General Council of the Bar of England and Wales.
Associated Word: Barrister (person).

Barrister (person): This is a type of lawyer in England and Wales. In the English legal system there are two types of lawyer. One type is called a solicitor and the other is called a barrister. A barrister will usually do the advocacy in a case after receiving instructions from the solicitor. Barristers are specifically trained in the skill of advocacy and legal procedure. They are famous for their court dress of long black gown and horsehair wig and are also known as "members of the Bar".
Associated Words: Advocacy (noun), Solicitor (person).

Bench (noun): This word is used to describe where judges sit in the courtroom. Historically, judges would sit on actual wooden benches and so the word was adopted for this meaning. It is also used in an abstract sense to describe a group of judges ("members of the bench").
Associated Word: Judge (person).

District Judge (person): A district judge is a judge that sits in the county court. They hear cases for breach of contract claims, tort claims, family law cases, etc. District judges are ex-solicitors or barristers and it is seen as a natural progression for many lawyers after years of legal practice.
Associated Words: Barrister (person), Contract Law (noun), County Court (noun), Solicitor (person), Tort Law (noun).

To Draft (verb): To draft is the legal word for "to write". In legal English the process of writing letters, contracts and other documents is called "drafting".
Associated Words: Drafted (past simple), Drafted (3rd form), Drafting (noun).

Immunity (noun): Immunity is the situation where a person cannot be taken to court for a crime (or a specific type of crime). This situation usually happens when someone is a member of a royal family, a politician, a diplomat or an ambassador. In legal English it is said that the person has immunity, or is immune from prosecution.
Associated Words: Immune (adjective), Court (noun).

Indemnity Insurance (noun): A lawyer must have indemnity insurance because if they make a mistake when they practise law, the insurance company will pay for any loss or damage that the lawyer's mistake has caused. It works in exactly the same way as car insurance when someone has an accident in his or her car. The insurance company will pay for the damage. Indemnity insurance is the same, but for lawyers.

In-House Lawyer (person): This is the name of a lawyer who works for a company or organisation rather than for a private practice law firm. Many large companies will have their own legal departments with their own lawyers (as well as instructing law firms). It is common for an in-house lawyer to qualify and practise in a law firm before moving to a legal department in a company or organisation. However, it is also possible to complete a training contract and qualify in-house.
Associated Word: To Qualify (verb).

Inns of Court (noun): These are professional associations for barristers in England and Wales. There are 4 associations in the Inns of Court: Middle Temple, Inner Temple, Gray's Inn and Lincoln's Inn. All barristers must be members of one of these Inns. The Inns of Court provide supervisory and disciplinary functions to its members and guide them from the student stage up to qualification. It is an old tradition that once a student barrister qualifies, they are "called" to the Bar by the Inn of which they are a member. A student barrister is more commonly known as a pupil. Student barristers must complete a pupillage before they are called to the Bar.

Associated Words: Barrister (person), To be Called to the Bar (collocation).

Judge (person): A judge is a person who hears cases in a court or tribunal. A judge's powers differ across different jurisdictions but their main role is to hear the evidence of the case, assess the credibility and strength of the parties' cases and to ensure a fair result. In some (more serious) criminal law cases a jury will give the verdict of the case. Usually, however, in most criminal and civil law cases, judges will give the verdict. A judge can sit alone in court or can be part of a panel of judges. In some criminal cases a judge is also called a magistrate.

Associated Words: Civil Law (noun), Court (noun), Criminal Law (noun), To Hear (verb), Jurisdiction (noun), Party (noun), Tribunal (noun), Verdict (noun).

Jury (noun): This word means the 12 members of the public who are chosen to decide the verdict in a trial. Juries are usually in the most serious criminal trials and some civil cases, especially those involving defamation proceedings. Jury trials are less popular in the English legal system as criminal trials for less serious offences are heard and decided by magistrates.

Associated Words: Defamation (noun), Verdict (noun).

The Law Society (noun): The Law Society of England and Wales is the organisation that represents solicitors (similar to the Bar Council who represent barristers). The main role of the Law Society is to provide guidance and support for practising solicitors and to those who want to train as a solicitor. All solicitors who practise law must be members of the Law Society.

Associated Words: Bar Council (noun), Barrister (person), To Practise (verb), Solicitor (person).

Layperson (person): This word is used to describe a person who is not a qualified lawyer or expert in a legal field. It is an informal word but it is

commonly used, especially in the world of legal English, as it is important that the layperson understands legal terms as well as the lawyers. A practical example of a layperson would be in a magistrate's court where one judge and two laypeople will sit on the bench, hear the case and decide the verdict.
Associated Words: Bench (noun), Verdict (noun).

Member of Parliament (person): A Member of Parliament (also known as an "MP") is a person who has been elected by the public to be a representative in the UK Government. An MP will sit in the House of Commons for one term of Parliament. A term of Parliament cannot be longer than 5 years. An MP's main role is to propose, debate and vote on bills in the House of Commons.
Associated Words: Bill (noun), Government (noun), House of Commons (noun).

Monarch (person): A monarch is the head of a monarchy. A monarchy is the form of government that rules a state or a country because power is passed down from their mother or father (the monarch "inherits" the title). The form of government in England and Wales is called a constitutional monarchy. This means that the country is ruled by an individual who receives power by inheritance.
Associated Words: Constitutional Monarchy (noun), To Inherit (verb), Monarchy (noun).

Notary Public (person): A notary public is a public officer whose main role is to serve members of the public in non-contentious matters. It is a document-based role including executing documents and witnessing and authorising statements. A notary public must complete special academic training and they will usually be a qualified solicitor or barrister.
Associated Words: Barrister (noun), Non-Contentious (noun), Solicitor (person), To Witness (verb).

Ombudsman (person): An ombudsman is an independent official who checks that the public are being served in the correct way. In relation to lawyers, there is a Legal Services Ombudsman where a member of the public can make complaints about their lawyer or law firm.

Partnership (noun): This word is used to describe the business structure of a law firm. Most law firms are formed as a partnership. The owners of the firm are the partners and these people own the law firm. Together these partners are called a partnership.

Peer (person): This is the name of a person who sits in the House of Lords. A peer will have a title (usually Lord for a man or Lady for a woman). They are then allowed to debate and vote on bills proposed by the House of Commons. Some peers are called "hereditary peers" which means that the title was given to them by their mother or father. Other peers are called "life peers" which means that the Monarch or the Prime Minister appointed them but they cannot pass their title on to their children.
Associated Words: Bill (noun), House of Commons (noun), House of Lords (noun), Monarchy (noun), Prime Minister (person).

To Practise (verb): Please note the spelling of this verb (with an "s"). In legal English this verb means to work as a lawyer. A lawyer will usually "practise" in a specialised area, for instance, litigation or mergers and acquisitions. It is important to note that the word "practice" with a "c" is the noun of the verb. The two words are pronounced exactly the same.
Associated Words: Practised (past simple), Practised (3rd form), Practised (adjective), Practice (noun).

Prime Minister (person): The Prime Minister is the most senior member of the Government, Cabinet and the Executive in England and Wales. The main role of the Prime Minister is to appoint members of the Cabinet and co-ordinate its activities and decisions. The Monarch appoints the Prime Minister after the votes of the general election have been counted. The Prime Minister is usually the leader of the political party who receives the most votes.
Associated Words: Cabinet (noun), Executive (noun), Government (noun), Monarch (person).

To Qualify (verb): This verb is used to describe the process of a trainee solicitor completing their training contract and becoming a solicitor. After completing the two-year training contract the trainee will qualify as a solicitor.

Associated Words: Qualified (past simple), Qualified (3rd form), Qualified (adjective), Qualification (noun), Solicitor (person), Training Contract (noun).

Queen's Counsel (person): This is the name given to a lawyer who has reached a very high level of practice in their area of law. Historically, they were invited to join this prestigious group of lawyers to advise the monarchy and used the letters "QC" after their name. If a lawyer is a QC it means that they have been appointed as an expert in their field and that they are experienced in their role as a barrister or a solicitor. If the monarch is a King, the letters change to "KC". They are also called "Silks" because they wear special silk gowns or cloaks in the courtroom.

Associated Words: Barrister (person), Solicitor (person).

Sole Practitioner (person): A sole practitioner is a lawyer who practises law on his or her own (without any partners or partnership). It is still very common, especially in smaller towns and villages, for lawyers to practise this way. Some sole practitioners specialise in one area of law and only practise in this field. Others will provide more general services especially in relation to private client work for individuals, for example, wills, divorces, conveyancing, etc.

Associated Words: Conveyancing (noun), Divorce (noun), Wills (noun).

Solicitor (person): A solicitor is a qualified legal advisor who has finished their law studies and practical training to become a lawyer in England and Wales. However, in England and Wales there are two types of lawyer (see barrister above). A solicitor gives legal advice, researches legal points, drafts letters and contracts and represents clients in court. The main difference between a barrister and a solicitor is that a solicitor needs a higher "right of audience" to represent clients in the higher courts, for example, the Court of Appeal. A right of audience is permission to represent and speak for your client in court. Barristers automatically have higher rights of audience.

Associated Words: Advocacy (noun), Barrister (person), Court (noun),

Court of Appeal (noun).

To Specialise (verb): This verb means that a lawyer chooses to work in a certain area of law to increase their expertise and knowledge. Usually lawyers specialise when they qualify after their training contract, but many lawyers also provide a general service and will advise clients on a number of areas.

Associated Words: Specialised (past simple), Specialised (3rd form), Specialised (adjective), Specialisation (noun), To Qualify (verb), Training Contract (noun).

Training Contract (noun): This is the name of the two-year working contract that a law graduate must complete to qualify as a solicitor. Before starting a training contract, a law graduate must complete the academic part of their training. The training contract is designed to introduce the law graduate to the practical training and working environment of a lawyer. Usually the training contract will consist of four seats or periods. Each seat is for six months in a different department in order for the trainee to gain experience in different areas of law. The trainee must complete at least 6 months in a contentious seat. Once the trainee successfully completes their training contract, they will become a qualified solicitor.

Associated Words: Contentious (adjective), To Qualify (verb), Solicitor (person).

To Undertake (verb): This verb is used in legal English when a solicitor formally promises to do something. For example, if a solicitor "gives an undertaking" to produce a document for the court, then the solicitor must produce that document or suffer possible consequences. Undertakings are seen as a principle of the code of conduct of a solicitor to act in good faith.

Associated Words: Undertook (past simple), Undertaken (3rd form), Undertaking (noun), Court (noun), Solicitor (person).

2. AREAS OF LAW

Administrative Law (noun): Administrative law deals with regulating the activity and decision making of government departments. One of its main areas is to check that each government department is acting within its power or authority. The courts can look at the decisions and activities of government departments and can decide if they were acting legally or not. This process is called judicial review.
Associated Words: Court (noun), Government (noun).

Banking and Finance (noun): This area of law deals with loans, funding, raising money and investment. It is one of the most profitable areas of law and is commonly practised by large international law firms all around the world.

Bankruptcy (noun): This word is very common in the English Legal System and describes the situation when the court declares that an individual, sole trader or partnership does not have enough money to pay its debts. This term is commonly misunderstood with the term insolvency. If you do not have enough money to pay all your debts, you are insolvent. You are bankrupt after the court officially declares that you are unable to pay all your debts. Also, the term bankruptcy is used in England and Wales only in relation to individuals, sole traders and partnerships. The term is not used in relation to companies in England and Wales.
Associated Words: Bankrupt (adjective), To Go Bankrupt (collocation), To Be Declared Bankrupt by the Court (collocation).

Civil Law (noun): There are two parts to the English legal system. One part is criminal law and the other is civil law. Civil law is the part of the English legal system that deals with the regulation of relationships between individuals and organisations where no crime has been committed. For instance, if Mr Smith has a contract with Mr Jones and Mr Smith does not do what the contract says he should, this is a civil law matter. No crime has been committed and so the argument between Mr Smith and Mr Jones will be dealt with by the rules and regulations of civil law. Civil law includes areas of law such as contract law, the law of tort, employment law and intellectual property law.

Associated Words: Contract Law (noun), Criminal Law (noun), Employment Law (noun), Intellectual Property Law (noun), The Law of Tort (noun).

Criminal Law (noun): This is the second part of the English legal system. The other part is civil law (above). Criminal law deals with the rules and regulations when a crime has been committed against the state. For instance, if Mr Smith enters Mr Jones's house late at night and takes Mr Jones's TV without Mr Jones's permission, Mr Smith will be dealt with by the criminal law system as he has committed the crime of burglary.

Associated Words: Civil Law (noun), To Commit (verb).

To Commit (verb): This is a very important verb in legal English. We use this verb when someone does something criminal or that is classed as a tort. For example, if someone steals something, then we say that have committed theft. If someone causes an accident, we say they have committed negligence (a type of tort). To commit is used with in both criminal law and civil law. It is not correct to say "to do/make theft" or "to do/make negligence". The correct verb to use is "to commit".

Associated Words: Committed (past simple), Committed (3rd form), Committed (adjective), Commission (noun), Tort (noun), To Steal (verb), Theft (noun), Negligence (noun).

Common Law (noun): Common law is a system of law developed by judicial decisions or judgments that become law when cases are decided. Common law is found in both civil law and criminal law. For centuries, judgments of the higher courts have been written down or "recorded" so that judges in the lower courts are able to follow the laws and principles decided previously. Common law uses the system of "binding precedents" which means that a lower court must follow the decisions and judgments of the higher courts. Only the higher courts can set precedents, such as the Supreme Court or the Court of Appeal. The common law system is completely separate from statute, but it is extremely important and is used every day in the courts to help decide cases.

Associated Words: Binding (adjective), Civil Law (noun), Court of Appeal (noun), Criminal Law (noun), Judgment (noun), Precedent (noun), Supreme Court (noun).

Company Law (noun): Company law covers all rules and regulations that a company must follow to operate legally. This is a very wide area of law and most law firms offer services to advise companies on their legal obligations. Common issues for Company Law lawyers are keeping accurate accounts, directors' obligations to the company, sending information to the Registrar of Companies (Companies House) and financing the company.
Associated Word: Obligations (noun).

Contentious (adjective): This word describes the type of work done by a lawyer or a law firm that involves arguments or disputes. For instance, lawyers who practise in litigation, divorce or personal injury cases practise contentious law. The opposite is non-contentious work, which includes buying and selling companies, conveyancing and drafting contracts.
Associated Words: Conveyancing (noun), Divorce (noun), To Draft (verb).

Contract Law (noun): This is the area of law that regulates the relationship between two or more people or "parties" who agree to buy something or to provide a type of service. Contract law is governed by both statute law and common law and is one of the largest areas of law in England and Wales. Contract law covers the rules about whether a contract actually exists, which parts of the contract are legally binding, the obligations of the parties, who has to pay money and how much, etc. There are thousands of cases in Common law that guide lawyers on the rules and principles of contract law in England and Wales.
Associated Words: Binding (adjective), Common Law (noun), Parties (noun), Statute (noun).

Conveyancing (noun): This is the area of law that deals with the buying, selling, transferring and registering of land or property. It is commonly used in relation to residential property, not commercial property. The verb "to convey" means to transfer or to send. The term conveyancing has been

adopted in legal English to mean the transfer of land. When somebody buys or sells a house in the UK they will employ the services of a conveyancing solicitor who will make sure that all the legal requirements are fulfiled for the transfer of the property. This includes reviewing the physical condition of the property, whether any third parties have rights over the property, the financial terms of the transfer and filing all necessary registrations with the authorities.
Associated Words: Rights (noun), Third Party (noun).

Defamation (noun): This is the name of the area of law that deals with negative statements. Defamation is the communication of a statement made by somebody about somebody else which causes this person to have a negative or worse image or reputation. Defamation can be divided into two areas: slander and libel (see below).
Associated Words: Slander (noun), Libel (noun).

Divorce (noun): This means that a married couple do not wish to continue living their lives together in a legal relationship. A divorce is a legal agreement to end the marriage and to decide future arrangements in relation to children, property, money and other assets that the couple own. In legal English we say that a couple "get a divorce" or "get divorced". This agreement must be accepted and approved by the court.
Associated Words: To Divorce (verb), To Get a Divorce (collocation), To Get Divorced (collocation), Court (noun).

Employment Law (noun): This area of law deals with the rules and regulations of workers (employees) and the companies or organisations they work for (employers). Employment law can be contentious or non-contentious. Contentious employment law includes issues such as unfair dismissal, discrimination, harassment, etc. Non-contentious employment law includes drafting employment contracts or drafting procedures for health and safety, etc.
Associated Words: Contentious (noun), To Draft (verb), Non-contentious (noun), Unfair Dismissal (noun).

Family Law (noun): This area of law deals with drafting agreements and resolving disputes in relation to married couples and children. Specialist

lawyers in this area advise clients in relation to separation, divorce, child custody and contact arrangements for parents, etc.
Associated Words: To Advise (verb), Divorce (noun), To Draft (verb), To Resolve (verb).

Insolvency Law (noun): This type of law deals with individuals and businesses that cannot pay their debts. A debt is money that must be paid to someone else. It is a very complicated area of law and there is a lot of legislation and common law that regulate what individuals and companies can do if they become insolvent.
Associated Words: Insolvent (adjective), Common Law (noun), Legislation (noun).

Intellectual Property Law (noun): Intellectual property law (IP law) deals with the protection and registration of rights over "intangible assets". An intangible asset is something you own which does not have any physical substance and is not monetary in nature. For example, a piece of music, a book or an article, art works, inventions, symbols and designs are intangible assets that can be protected under IP Law. Some of the IP rights that can be given (or granted) to these assets are copyright, trademarks, patents, industrial design rights and in some situations trade secrets. **Associated Word:** Rights (noun).

Immigration Law (noun): Immigration law deals with the policies and rules of a government in relation to the movement of foreign nationals entering their country. Such policies include the legal status of foreign nationals, citizenship and access to social benefits.

To Inherit (verb): This verb means that someone receives assets from a relative or a friend after that relative or friend has died. It is common in the English Legal System for this process to be done with a "will". Other examples of using the verb inherit are, the Monarch inheriting the title of King or Queen and a hereditary peer inheriting the title of Lord. or Lady.
Associated Words: Inherited (past simple), Inherited (3rd form), Inherited (adjective), Inheritance (noun), Monarch (person), Peer (person), Will (noun).

Landlord and Tenant Law (noun): This area of law is related to the rights of a person living in a house or flat that they do not own. The person who lives in the property is called a tenant and the person who owns the property is called a landlord. The Tenant's obligations are usually to pay rent to the landlord and keep the property in good condition. The landlord's obligations include repairing anything that is broken, etc.
Associated Word: Obligations (noun).

Libel (noun): This is a type of defamation. Libel is the written or broadcast communication of a false statement that makes a person or organisation's reputation or image worsen.
Associated Word: Defamation (noun).

Mergers and Acquisitions (noun): This area of law is commonly called "M&A". It deals with buying and selling of companies, businesses and their assets. A merger is when two or more companies join together and continue as one company. An acquisition is when one company takes control of another (a takeover). It is a very profitable area of law and is popular with the larger law firms, especially the magic circle firms.
Associated Words: Magic Circle (noun).

Non-Contentious (adjective): Non-contentious work is the opposite of contentious work. It means that a lawyer practises an area of law that is not based on a dispute. For example, a merger of two companies, buying or selling a house and writing a will are non-contentious areas of law.
Associated Words: Contentious (adjective), To Practise (verb), Will (noun).

Real Estate Law (noun): This area of law deals with the buying, selling, leasing and registration of property and land. The phrase is generally used for commercial property transactions but can also be used for residential property work.

Slander (noun): Slander is one of two types of defamation. Slander deals with the spoken communication of a statement about a person or organisation that creates a worse or negative image or reputation.
Associated Word: Defamation (noun).

Tax Law (noun): This area of law deals with the calculation, planning and payment of different taxes in a specific jurisdiction. It is a very complex and complicated area of law and there are many statutes and common law precedents that regulate how, when and how much tax each individual or organisation must pay to the government.

Associated Words: Common Law (noun), Government (noun), Jurisdiction (noun), Statute (noun).

Tort Law/The Law of Tort (noun): The law of tort relates to "civil wrongs". It is unique in nature as you do not need to have a contract with someone for the law of tort to operate. In the law of tort there are situations when we owe a duty of care to other people (who we may not even know). In these situations we must be careful not to cause or create any injury or damage in these situations. As you can imagine, it is a very popular area of law and there are thousands of common law cases and precedents that have developed the law of Tort over hundreds of years. Tort law includes negligence (carelessness), nuisance (stopping someone having quiet enjoyment of their home), defamation (slander and libel), false imprisonment and trespass (to land and to the person). It is a common law principle and is designed to compensate the victim. It is not designed to punish the person who caused the tort (also known as a "tortfeasor").

Associated Words: Common Law (noun), Defamation (noun), Libel (noun), Slander (noun), Precedent (noun).

Trust Law/The Law of Trusts (noun): Trust Law is a very complicated area of law. It deals with the ownership and control of property and how that property is managed. The simplest way to explain trust law is with an example. Let's say that Mr Smith owns some land and property. Mr Smith has a grandson called Thomas. Thomas is 4 years old. Mr Smith would like to give Thomas the land and property but not until Thomas is 18 years old. However, Mr Smith is not in good health and so would like someone else to manage the land and property for him. He has a good friend Mr Jones who can look after the property until Thomas is 18 years old. In this situation Mr Smith will create a trust. He will transfer the land and property to Mr Jones. Mr Jones will keep the land and property for Thomas until Thomas is 18. When Thomas is 18, Mr Jones will transfer the land and property to Thomas.

In this situation, Mr Smith is called the "settlor". Mr Jones is called the "trustee" and he manages the land and property for Mr Smith. Thomas is the "beneficiary" of the trust and will receive the land and property when he is 18 years old.

Will (noun): A will is a document in which a person explains who and where they would like their property to go to after they die. Usually the document is entitled "Last Will and Testament" and must be signed by the testator (the person whose will it is) and witnessed. It is not necessary for a will to be drafted by a lawyer but it is generally advised that it should be. If a person dies without a will then there are special rules that will decide where the property will go. These are called intestacy rules.

Associated Words: To Draft (verb), To Witness (verb).

3. THE COURTS

Admiralty Court (noun): This court is part of the High Court of Justice and hears maritime law and shipping cases. For example, if there is a dispute over contract where the transportation of goods is by ship, the Admiralty Court may hear the case. The Admiralty Court has jurisdiction to hear both criminal law and civil law cases.
Associated Words: Contract Law (noun), Civil Law (noun), Criminal Law (noun), High Court (noun), Jurisdiction (noun).

Advocacy (noun): The term advocacy is used for the skill of speaking and presenting your case in a court or tribunal. It is common for a barrister to conduct the advocacy in English courts, but solicitors can also do this. Law students who want to be a barrister or a solicitor will receive special training in advocacy at law school or college.
Associated Words: Advocate (person), Barrister (person), Solicitor (person).

To Appeal (verb): To appeal means to ask a higher court or tribunal to review a decision or judgment to reverse or overrule part or all of it. There are many reasons why a judgment is appealed. For example, it could be appealed because the judge(s) made a mistake with the law or because new evidence has appeared in the case. The process for appealing is simple. Usually, a special application or request is made to the court. In some cases permission (or "leave") of the court must be obtained to allow the application. If the appeal is allowed, the appellate court will hear the case again. The party who applies for the appeal is called the appellant and the other party is called the respondent.
Associated Words: Appealed (past simple), Appealed (3rd form), Appealed (adjective), Appeal (noun), Appellant (noun), Appellate Court (noun), Court (noun), Evidence (noun), To Hear (verb), Judgment (noun), Party (noun), Respondent (noun).

Appellate Court (adjective): This is the general name given to the courts that hear appeals. For instance, the Court of Appeal will hear an appeal from a High Court judgment. In this situation the Court of Appeal is the appellate court. If the judgment from the Court of Appeal is appealed, the Supreme Court will hear the appeal. The Court of Appeal and the Supreme Court are both appellate courts for both civil and criminal cases.

Associated Words: To Appeal (verb), Civil Law (noun), Court of Appeal (noun), Criminal Law (noun), High Court (noun), Judgment (noun), Supreme Court (noun).

To Bind (verb): This means that a law (common or statute) must be obeyed and followed. It is used in common law where, for example, a court of first instance must follow the decisions of higher courts (the doctrine of precedent). Common law in the English Legal System is one of the most important parts of the law. Rulings or judgments of the higher courts create precedents. These precedents "bind" the lower courts. This means that the lower courts must follow the principles of law set by the higher courts. In legal English it is said that the precedent is "binding", meaning it must be followed.

Associated Words: Bound (past simple), Bound (3rd form), Binding (adjective), To be Bound by Precedent/the Court (collocation), Court of First Instance (noun), Common Law (noun), Judgment (noun), Precedent (noun).

Chancery Division (noun): This court is part of the High Court of Justice in England and Wales and specialises in hearing cases on company law, tax law and insolvency law.

Associated Words: High Court (noun), Company Law (noun), Insolvency Law (noun), Tax Law (noun).

Court (noun): A court is the place where lawyers, judges and juries will discuss and decide how to resolve a dispute or whether a crime has been committed or not. The word "court" is used to describe both i) the physical building in which both civil law and criminal law cases are heard and adjudged, and ii) the judges and the institution generally. You will often hear the word court used in both contexts.

Associated Words: To Commit (verb), Civil Law (noun), Criminal Law (noun), Judge (person), Trial by Jury (noun).

Commercial Court (noun): The Commercial Court is a specialist division of the High Court of Justice. As the name suggests, it is used to hear commercial law cases, for instance, banking or insurance law.
Associated Words: Banking (noun), To Hear (verb), High Court (noun), Tax Law (noun).

County Court (noun): Each region or district in England and Wales has a local court. This court is called a county court. A county court is used to hear common everyday cases such as small contract claims, personal injury claims, divorces, etc. Usually the claims are not worth a lot of money in the county court because higher value claims are dealt with by the High Court in London.
Associated Words: Contract Law (noun), Divorce (noun), High Court (noun).

Court of Appeal (noun): This is the name of the court that is one step up from the High Court in civil cases and the Crown Court for criminal cases. Therefore, the Court of Appeal has both a Civil Division and a Criminal Division. As the name suggests the main role is to hear appeals from the lower courts and (if necessary) send even more complicated cases to the Supreme Court. Both the Supreme Court and the Court of Appeal may set binding precedents, which must be followed by the lower courts.
Associated Words: Binding (adjective), High Court (noun), Precedent (noun), Supreme Court (noun).

Court of First Instance (noun): This name is given to the courts that hear a case first. This can mean a County Court or High Court for civil claims or a Magistrates Court for criminal cases. These courts cannot set precedents but instead must follow precedents from the Court of Appeal and the Supreme Court.
Associated Words: County Court (noun), Court of Appeal (noun), High Court (noun), Precedent (noun), Supreme Court (noun).

To Dissent (verb): This verb is used with judgments of the court. A dissenting judgment is a judgment from a judge that does not agree with the majority decision of the other judges in that case. For instance, in the Court of Appeal it is usual for three judges to hear the case. Two of the judges may find in favour of the appellant, and so by a majority the appellant wins the case. However, one judge may not agree with the other two judges and decides against the appellant. This judge is called a dissenting judge and his judgment is called a dissenting judgment. His judgment does not have any effect because he is in the minority, but it is made public that he disagrees with the majority of the court. The appellant would still win the case, even if there were a dissenting judgment. Dissenting judgments can arise because the judges disagree on a point of law or the interpretation of a precedent. **Associated Words:** Dissented (past simple), Dissented (3rd form), Dissenting (adjective), Court of Appeal (noun), Judge (person), Judgment (noun).

To Distinguish (verb): This verb is used when the court does not have to follow a binding precedent. When a lawyer wishes to rely on a precedent of the court, the court has two options. First, it may decide that the precedent is relevant to the case and so the court is "bound" by the precedent and must follow it. Alternatively, the court may think that the precedent that the lawyer wishes to rely on is not relevant or connected to the case it is hearing now. In this situation, the court will "distinguish" the precedent from the case and will decide that the court does not need to follow the precedent. Usually, precedents are distinguished from cases because the facts are not similar enough, or the legal arguments are too different. **Associated Words:** Distinguished (past simple), Distinguished (3rd form), Distinguished (adjective), To Bind (verb), Court (noun), Precedent (noun).

Family Division (noun): This is a department of the High Court of Justice in England and Wales. As the name suggests, the department deals with all cases and claims in relation to family law. For example, the court will hear divorce proceedings and proceedings for the custody of children. **Associated Words:** Divorce (noun), Family Law (noun), High Court (noun).

High Court of Justice in England and Wales (noun): This court is usually referred to as the "High Court". It is the court of first instance for high value and important claims. The court is divided into three divisions: the Family

Division, the Queen's Bench Division and the Chancery Division. The court is located in London in the Royal Courts of Justice. The High Court only hears civil claims (criminal cases are not heard there).

Associated Words: Chancery Division (noun), Civil Law (noun), Court (noun), Criminal Law (noun), Family Division (noun), Queen's Bench Division (noun), Royal Courts of Justice (noun).

To Hear (verb): In legal English this verb has the meaning of listening to the advocates in court. For example, "the case will be heard next Monday at 12pm" The noun is "Hearing". The word hearing is very common in legal English and it is used when the advocates and judge(s) meet in court to discuss the case. For example, "the hearing is scheduled for 12ᵗʰ March".

Associated Words: Heard (past simple), Heard (3ʳᵈ form), Hearing (noun), Advocate (person), Court (noun), Judge (person).

To Impose (verb): This means that a situation is placed, put or forced on someone. For example the government will impose taxes on the public, or for use in criminal law, the court or judge will impose a sentence on the defendant if the jury reaches a verdict of guilty.

Associated Words: Imposed (past simple), Imposed (3ʳᵈ form), Imposed (adjective), Court (noun), Judge (noun), Jury (noun), To Reach a Verdict (collocation).

Jurisdiction (noun): This word is used to describe when a court has the authority or right to hear and decide cases in that area of law and in that location. In legal English lawyers say that the court "has jurisdiction" to hear the case. For example, only the Court of Appeal and the Supreme Court have jurisdiction to hear Appeal cases in England and Wales. This means that they have the authority or the right to hear these cases.

Associated Words: To have Jurisdiction (collocation), Court (noun), To Hear (verb), Right (noun).

Judgment (noun): A judgment is a decision, finding or ruling of a court or a tribunal. It is used in different contexts in the English Legal System. Firstly, a judgment of the court can mean the decision of who won the case. A common collocation is "The court found judgment in favour of the claimant". Another collocation is "to hand down judgment" which means to give judgment. Secondly, the word judgment refers to the document written by the judge or judges to explain their decision. Judgments can be as short as one page, but have also reached over 100 pages long. Please note the spelling: "judgment" with no "e" is the legal spelling as described above. "Judgement" is the general word for assessing something, for example "I used my judgement to decide what television to buy". Here the word judgement is not being used in a legal context and so is spelt with an "e".

Associated Words: To Find Judgment in Favour of (collocation), To Hand Down Judgment (collocation), Court (noun), Tribunal (noun).

Law Reports (noun): Law reports are a large collection of judgments from many different courts in the Legal English System. At first, law reports were only available in hard copy paper form but nowadays most are on the Internet. The law reports come in different groups and categories and are fundamental for barristers and solicitors to find precedents and to research other important information.

Associated Words: Barrister (person), Judgment (noun), Precedent (noun), Solicitor (person).

Obiter Dictum (noun): This phrase is Latin for "said in passing" and in legal English refers to the part or parts of a judgment that are not the ratio decidendi (see below). The Obiter Dictum part of the judgment usually consists of the history of the case and the facts and law used to argue the issues.

Associated Words: Judgment (noun), Ratio Decidendi (noun).

To Overrule (verb): This verb is used to mean that an appellate court or tribunal has decided against an earlier decision or verdict and reverses or changes it.

Associated Words: Overruled (past simple), Overruled (3rd form), Appellate Court (noun), To Reverse (verb), Tribunal (noun), Verdict (noun).

Precedent – meaning 1 of 2 (noun): This meaning of the word precedent is in relation to common law. Historically, judgments of the courts were written down (known as "recorded"). Over the centuries that followed, a system of following the decisions of the higher courts became usual practice. Nowadays the system of following precedents is one of the most important doctrines of the English Legal System. The process is fairly simple. The judgments of the higher courts (Supreme Court and Court of Appeal) must be followed by the lower courts (High Court, County Court, etc). For example, if there is a case about a dispute over a point of law, the lawyers will check the records of the Supreme Court and the Court of Appeal to see if there is a ruling from these courts that will tell them what was decided in similar cases before. If the facts and situations of the cases are very similar then the court must follow this precedent. If the facts and situation are not so similar then the court does not have to follow the precedent. Each judgment will have a part called the "ratio decidendi". This is the part of the judgment, which forms the precedent and the part that should be followed by the lower courts. This is the doctrine of "binding precedents".

Associated Words: To Bind (verb), Court of Appeal (noun), County Court (noun), High Court (noun), Judgment (noun), Ratio Decidendi (noun), Supreme Court (noun).

Party (noun): A party to proceedings is a person or organisation who has an interest in those proceedings. Usually this means that there will be a claimant (the person who starts the claim) or a defendant (the person who defends the claim) and maybe a third party (a person with an interest in the claim). If a person or organisation is named in the proceedings as a claimant, defendant or third party then they are a "party" to the claim. **Associated Words:** Claim (noun), Claimant (noun), Defendant (noun), Proceedings (noun), Third Party (noun).

To Prove (verb): This verb means that someone is trying to establish that something is true or genuine. In criminal law the prosecution must prove that the defendant is guilty. The defendant does not have to prove they are innocent. In civil cases the claimant or defendant must prove their case on the balance of probabilities. This means that they must show the court that their version of the case is more probable or likely than the other party. **Associated Words:** Proved (past simple), Proved/Proven (3rd form),

Proved/Proven (adjective) Proof (noun), Court (noun), Party (noun).

Queen's Bench Division (noun): This is a division of the High Court of Justice in England and Wales and has two main functions. The first function is that it hears regular civil cases in relation to tort and contract law. The second function is that it acts as a supervisory court for the lower courts. It is also where the Administrative Court sits, so this division will also hear all Judicial Review proceedings. The name of the division is dependent on the gender of the Monarch (the name changes to King's Bench Division if there is a male Monarch).
Associated Words: Administrative Court (noun), Contract Law (noun), High Court (noun), Tort Law (noun).

Ratio Decidendi (noun): This Latin phrase (which means "the reason for the decision") is the part of a judgment that gives us the precedent. Every judgment in a court in the English Legal System is made of two parts. The Ratio Decidendi is the most important part as it is the part of the judgment where the judge explains the reason for their decision. The rest of the judgment is called the Obiter Dictum. It is very important in Common Law to find and understand the Ratio Decidendi of a case as it is this that forms the precedent and binds lower courts.
Associated Words: Common Law (noun), Judge (person), Judgment (noun), Obiter Dictum (noun), Precedent (noun).

To Resolve (verb): This verb means to solve a problem or dispute to the satisfaction of, or to the agreement of, everyone involved. It is commonly used in legal English in relation to ending a dispute or court proceedings.
Associated Words: Resolved (past simple), Resolved (3rd form), Resolved (adjective), Resolution (noun), Court (noun).

The Royal Courts of Justice (noun): The Royal Courts of Justice is the building on The Strand in London where the High Court and Court of Appeal sit. It was built in the 1870s and is open to the public (but some cases will be private). It generally deals with civil law cases, but the Court of Appeal will hear criminal appeals. It should not be confused with the Central Criminal Court (also known as The Old Bailey), which is about 1 kilometre to the east.

Associated Words: Civil Law (noun), Court of Appeal (noun), High Court (noun).

To Reverse (verb): In legal English the verb to reverse is used when an Appellate Court disagrees with the original judgment and "reverses" the decision. For example, if a claimant wins their case in the High Court, the defendant has the right to appeal the decision to the Court of Appeal. If this appeal is allowed, the Court of Appeal will hear the case again. If the Court of Appeal believes that the defendant should win the case, they will reverse the original judgment of the High Court.

Associated Words: Reserved (past simple), Reversed (3rd form), Reversed (adjective), Reversal (noun), To Appeal (verb), Appellate Court (noun), Court of Appeal (noun), High Court (noun).

Supreme Court (noun): The Supreme Court is the highest court in England and Wales. It is the ultimate appellate court and can hear appeals from all of the courts in England and Wales. Before 2009 the highest court was in the House of Lords, but this was moved and re-named the Supreme Court. The Court has jurisdiction over all areas of law in England and Wales.

Associated Words: Appellate Court (noun), House of Lords (noun), Jurisdiction (noun).

To Sue (verb): This is the one of the most common verbs in the Legal English System and it means to go to court or to start legal proceedings. It is an informal word and so you are more likely to hear the phrase "issue proceedings" in a formal legal environment. To sue someone for something is a common collocation, for example, "Mr Smith sued Mr Jones for negligence".

Associated Words: Sued (past simple), Sued (3rd form), To Sue Someone for Something (collocation), Court (noun).

Technology and Construction Court (noun): This court is a specialised court that, as the name suggests, deals primarily with technology and construction disputes. It is a division of the Queen's Bench Division (which is part of the High Court of Justice). It has recently seen a large increase in case load due to the development of the Internet and has a growing reputation for expertise and knowledge in this area and for resolving disputes of a technological nature.

Associated Words: High Court (noun), Queen's Bench Division (noun), To Resolve (verb).

Tribunal (noun): A tribunal is a type of court. Generally in legal English we use the word court for the place where disputes are heard, however, in some fields the correct term to use would be tribunal. One of the most common areas in the English legal system that uses the term tribunal is employment law.

Associated Words: Court (noun), Employment Law (noun).

To Uphold (verb): This verb is the opposite of the verb "to reverse" or "to overrule". It means that an appellate court has heard the appeal and agrees with the verdict of the lower court. For example "The appellate court upheld the original verdict".

Associated Words: Upheld (past simple), Upheld (3rd form), Upheld (adjective), Appeal (noun), Appellate Court (noun), To Reverse (verb), To Overrule (verb), Verdict (noun).

Verdict (noun): This word means the decision of the judge or jury in a civil or criminal trial. The decision is final unless the verdict is successfully appealed in a higher court. It is common to use the phrase "to reach a verdict" which means to decide a verdict.

Associated Words: To Appeal (verb), Civil Law (noun), Criminal Law (noun), Judge (person), Jury (noun).

To Witness (verb): This verb is one of the most commonly used in the English Legal System and means that a person has seen, heard, read or knows something of interest to a case. The system relies on witnesses to describe their version of events or situations to the court. The judge or jury then reach a verdict based on the evidence given by the witnesses.

Associated Words: Witnessed (past simple), Witnessed (3rd form), Witnessed (adjective), Witness (person), Court (noun), Evidence (noun), Jury (noun), Verdict (noun).

4. PARLIAMENT

Act of Parliament (noun): An act of parliament is a piece of legislation that comes from the process of the UK Parliament voting in favour of a proposed law. A proposed law is also called a "bill". The bill begins in the House of Commons and is debated by the Members of Parliament. The House of Lords will also debate the content of the bill to decide if they agree that it should be UK law. After members of parliament vote (and pass) the bill, it is signed by the King or Queen. This is called "royal assent". Once the act receives royal assent, the act will "come into force" and it becomes a new law.

Associated Words: Bill (noun), To Come into Force (collocation), House of Commons (noun), House of Lords (noun), Members of Parliament (noun), Royal Assent (noun).

To Ban (verb): This means that something is stopped, prohibited or forbidden. It is commonly used for situations where, in the past something was allowed or legal, and then some point later it was made illegal or not allowed. Parliament uses legislation to ban various actions or behaviour. For example, Parliament has banned smoking in public restaurants, bars and clubs.

Associated Words: Banned (past simple), Banned (3rd form), Banned (adjective), Ban (noun), Parliament (noun).

Bill (noun): This word is used for a proposed law that is being drafted or debated before Parliament. When a law is proposed it is written as a draft and debated by both the House of Commons and the House of Lords. If both houses approve the bill then it is passed to the monarch who will give the bill royal assent. Once the bill has been given royal assent the bill becomes an act of parliament.

Associated Words: Act (noun), To Draft (noun), House of Commons (noun), House of Lords (noun), Monarch (person), Parliament (noun) Royal Assent (noun).

By-Election (noun): A by-election is a type of election that is held if a member of parliament leaves their position as a politician and has to be replaced. The most common reasons for this are if the MP dies, resigns or retires.
Associated Words: Election (noun), Member of Parliament (person).

By-Law (noun): By-laws are local laws and regulations that a local authority can pass without the need for a bill to go through parliament. By-laws will only affect local issues and so parliament allows local authorities to regulate these laws.
Associated Words: Bill (noun), Parliament (noun).

Cabinet (noun): This is the name given to the group of members of parliament (MPs) who are in control of the most important departments in the government. The cabinet is part of the executive and so, under the doctrine of the separation of powers, is kept away from the legislature and the judiciary. Examples of members of the cabinet are the Prime Minister, the Home Secretary, the Chancellor of the Exchequer, the Minister for Education and the Minister for Health.
Associated Words: Government (noun), Judiciary (noun), Legislature (noun), Member of Parliament (person).

Constitutional Monarchy (noun): This term is used to describe the political system for the UK. Many believe that the UK is a pure democracy, however, the UK has an unelected monarch and all laws that come into force must receive royal assent from the King or Queen. Due to this, the UK is not a pure democracy although in practice no monarch has refused to give royal assent for centuries.
Associated Words: To Come into Force (collocation), Royal Assent (noun).

To Come into Force (collocation): This phrase is used to describe the situation when a proposed law has legal effect. It is the final step of a proposed piece of legislation that has been debated in parliament, voted on, passed and received Royal Assent. This phrase is only used with statutes. It is not used in common law.
Associated Words: Came into Force (past simple), Come into Force (3rd

form), Common Law (noun), Legislation (noun), Parliament (noun), To Pass (verb), Royal Assent (noun), Statute (noun).

Delegated Legislation (noun): This is the name given to legislation that is passed by local authorities and other regulatory organisations. The UK Parliament may give these authorities and organisations the power to make their own laws that are specific to their area. This means that the role of passing legislation is "delegated" to these authorities and organisations. By-laws (see above) are a type of delegated legislation. Such powers usually relate to local laws and regulations in relation to roads, local taxes, etc.
Associated Words: By-laws (noun), Parliament (noun), To Pass (verb).

Devolution (noun): This means that a country or state who is a part of a group of countries or states want to be separate or independent from the group. An example is Wales, who have devolved some powers of their own government away from the government of Great Britain. They are able to make some decisions in relation to the law in Wales without any influence from the British Government. However, they are not fully independent of Great Britain, as some decisions will still be made by the British Government.
Associated Words: To Devolve (verb), Devolved (adjective), Government (noun).

Election (noun): An election is an organised voting event. The term is usually used to describe the process of deciding which person or party is the most popular with the public and so will win the majority of votes to take a position of authority or power. The term General Election is used in the UK to describe the event of voting for the national government. Local elections are also held regularly and will decide whom and which party will control the local governments around the country.
Associated Words: General Election (noun), Government (noun).

General Election (noun): This is the word used for the main UK parliamentary elections that are held in the UK every 5 years. This election decides which person will be a member of parliament and will represent each area of the UK. The political party with a majority of members of parliament in the House of Commons will form the government.

Associated Words: Government (noun), House of Commons (noun), Member of Parliament (person).

Government (noun): The Government in the UK is the organisation that has been elected by the public in a general election. They are responsible for running the country and serving the public. Usually the government is one political party who won the highest number of votes in the general election. The government is part of the executive and is also responsible for the implementation of the law.
Associated Words: Executive (noun), General Election (noun), To Implement (verb).

Green Paper (noun): This phrase is used to describe an early version of a proposed law (or bill). It is an early stage of the legislative process. The document will be presented to parliament and it will be debated and discussed after listening to advice and recommendations. If the Green Paper is generally supported by parliament then it will become a White Paper that is the next stage of the legislative process.
Associated Words: Advice (noun), Bill (noun), Parliament (noun), White Paper (noun).

House of Commons (noun): This is the name of the lower house of the Houses of Parliament. The second is the House of Lords. The House of Commons is the house where the members of parliament sit, debate and vote on proposed legislation. It is a democratic institution because the public elects each MP. Each proposed law (or bill) is voted on and then sent to the House of Lords for review and approval.
Associated Words: Bill (noun), Houses of Parliament (noun), House of Lords (noun), Legislation (noun).

House of Lords (noun): This is the higher house of the Houses of Parliament. Unlike the House of Commons, the members of the House of Lords are not elected. Instead the members are either "hereditary peers" which means that their title was passed down to them by their father or mother, or they are "life peers" which means that they were appointed (by the King or Queen). Before 1911 the House of Lords had the power to reject legislation proposed by the House of Commons. Since then they only have the power to delay the progress of the proposed bill. The main role of the House of Lords is to advise and provide guidance to the House of Commons. **Associated Words:** To Advise (verb), Bill (noun), House of Commons (noun), Houses of Parliament (noun).

Houses of Parliament (noun): This is the more common name for the Palace of Westminster. It consists of two houses, the House of Commons and the House of Lords and is the home of the legislature of England and Wales.
Associated Words: House of Commons (noun), House of Lords (noun), Legislature.

Hansard (noun): This is the official record of the spoken debates in the House of Commons and the House of Lords. All questions, answers and statements are recorded and made public the following day.
Associated Words: House of Commons (noun), House of Lords (noun).

Home Office (noun): This is a government department that manages security issues in the UK. The Home Office is responsible for the Police, UK Border Agency, immigration, Security Service (MI5) and counter-terrorism. The cabinet minister who is in charge of the Home Office is known as the Home Secretary.
Associated Word: Government (noun)

Hung Parliament (noun): This phrase is used to describe the situation when no political party has an overall majority in the House of Commons. To have a majority, one political party must have over 50% of the total number of MPs in the House of Commons. If no party has over 50% then the situation is called a Hung Parliament. If this happens, usually the party with the most MPs will then try to join together with a smaller party so that, together, they have over 50% of the total of number MPs. This is called a "Coalition".
Associated Words: House of Commons (noun).

To Implement (verb): This verb is often used in the English legal system and it means to start or to introduce something. The verb is used with new legislation coming into force. For example, European Union law will need to be implemented into the law of each member state, which means that it is necessary for national governments to introduce these laws in a similar way.

Associated Words: Implemented (past simple), Implemented (3rd form), Implemented (adjective), Implementation (noun), European Union Law (noun), Legislation (noun).

Legislation (noun): Legislation is a general word for laws, statutes and acts of parliament. The word is used to confirm that a law has come into force and has been approved by parliament and the monarchy. It is important to remember that in the English Legal System, legislation only comes from Parliament (the legislature). The courts do not introduce legislation, but rather check that the legislation is interpreted correctly. As a point of grammar, legislation is already plural and uncountable. To use legislation as a countable noun, you can use the collocation "pieces of legislation".

Associated Words: Act of Parliament (noun), To Come Into Force (noun), Legislature (noun), Monarchy, (noun), Parliament (noun), Statute (noun).

Member of Parliament (person): A member of parliament (MP) is a person who has been voted by the public to be their representative in the UK Government. An MP sits in the House of Commons. They are only elected for one term of Parliament, which is a maximum of 5 years. Once they become an MP they can sit in the House of Commons and propose, debate and vote on bills.

Associated Words: Bills (noun), Government (noun), House of Commons (noun), House of Lords (noun), Parliament (noun), Term (noun).

Monarch (person): The form of government in England and Wales is called a constitutional monarchy (as explained above). This means that the country is ruled by an individual who receives power by way of inheritance. We call this person a monarch but it is more commonly known as the King or Queen.

Associated Words: Constitutional Monarchy (noun).

Parliament (noun): Parliament is responsible for the legislation in England and Wales. The word parliament is used to describe the two chambers (House of Commons and House of Lords) who propose, debate and vote on new law and amend laws already in existence. Parliament sits in the Palace of Westminster (also known as the Houses of Parliament) next to the river Thames in London.

Associated Words: House of Commons (noun), House of Lords (noun), Legislation (noun).

To Pass (verb): This verb is used to describe the process of approving legislation in parliament. For instance it is commonly used for laws that have been agreed by both houses in parliament and will then be given royal assent. Once royal assent has been given (when the monarch signs the bill), the new law is passed. It is not the same as "to come into force" as a law can pass on one date but not actually come into force until a later date.

Associated Words: Passed (past simple), Passed (3rd form), Passed (adjective), Bill (noun), To Come into Force (collocation), Legislation (noun), Monarch (person), Parliament (noun), Royal Assent (noun).

Peer (person): This is the name of a person who sits in the House of Lords. A peer will have a title (usually Lord for a man or Lady for a woman). They are then allowed to debate and vote on bills proposed by the House of Commons. Some peers are called "hereditary peers" which means that the title was given to them by their mother or father. Other peers are called "life peers" which means that the monarchy or the Prime Minister appointed them but they cannot pass their title on to their children.

Associated Words: Bill (noun), House of Commons (noun), House of Lords (noun), Monarchy (noun), Prime Minister (person).

To Repeal (verb): This verb is used when parliament cancels or stops an existing law from having legal effect. For example, if an existing act of parliament is seen to be old and not suitable for modern times then parliament can "repeal" the act and stop it from having legal effect. It can replace it the act with a more modern version or simply cancel it. Acts of parliament can be repealed in full (so all of the act is cancelled) or partially repealed (only parts of the act are cancelled).

Associated Words: Repealed (past simple), Repealed (3rd form), Act of Parliament (noun), Parliament (noun).

Royal Assent (noun): This is the last past in the process of a bill becoming an act. A bill will first travel through the House of Common and the House of Lords. Once both houses have voted and passed the bill, it will be sent to the monarch for their signature to obtain royal assent. Once the monarch has signed the bill, it becomes an act of parliament. It may not be in force immediately, but it is now an act. It is legal for a monarch to refuse to sign an act, but in practice a monarch has not refused to give royal assent for centuries.
Associated Words: To Give Royal Assent (collocation), Act of Parliament (noun), Bill (noun), House of Commons (noun), House of Lords (noun), Monarch (person).

Secondary Legislation (noun): This is also known as delegated legislation. This is law that is passed by an executive or local authority without having to go through parliament. This power will be given to them by parliament and it is common in relation to local authorities making decisions and passing laws locally.
Associated Words: Delegated Legislation (noun), Parliament (noun).

Statute (noun): This word means the same as an act of parliament and together with legislation is one of the three ways of describe laws made by the legislature.
Associated Words: Act of Parliament (noun), Legislation (noun), Legislature (noun).

Statutory Instrument (noun): A statutory instrument is a type of secondary legislation that supports the main acts of parliament. They can be delegated to ministers and government departments or they can provide further rules and regulations of an act.
Associated Words: Act of Parliament (noun), Government (noun), Secondary Legislation (noun).

White Paper (noun): This document is produced by the government to present their proposals for a bill. This document would have previously been a Green Paper (see above) and after receiving comments and opinion a White Paper will then be produced. After further comments and opinions, the White Paper will be amended and will finally become a bill to be voted on in parliament.

Associated Words: Bill (noun), Government (noun), Green Paper (noun).

5. EUROPEAN LAW

Council of the European Union (noun): Please note that this is not the same as the European Council (below). The Council of the European Union, together with the European Parliament and European Commission are the main legislative organisations of the European Union. Their roles are different depending on the type of legislation they are proposing but usually this Council will debate and vote on proposed laws from the European Commission. In this sense, the Council has a similar role to the European Parliament.
Associated Words: European Commission (noun), European Parliament (noun), Legislation (noun).

Directive (noun): A directive is a type of European Union law. Each member state must implement each European directive, but they can do this by using their own method of implementation. The principle and the particular aims and results of the directive must be the same as the European Union intended, but member states are free to implement the legislation themselves.
Associated Words: European Union law (noun).

European Commission (noun): This is an organisation based in Brussels, Belgium that proposes what laws are needed for the member states of the European Union, how they are implemented and to make sure that the European treaties are followed.
Associated Words: European Union law (noun), Treaty (noun).

European Court of Human Rights (noun): This court was created by the European Convention on Human Rights. It is not an organisation of the European Union and is not binding on the member states as law. However, it hears cases and advises member states and individuals on whether they are in breach of the Convention on Human Rights.
Associated Words: To Advise (verb), Binding (adjective), To Hear (verb).

European Court of Justice (noun): This court hears cases on European Union law and whether member states of the European Union have interpreted European law correctly. It also hears disputes between individuals and companies against governments of the EU states.
Associated Words: European Union Law (noun), To Hear (verb).

European Council (noun): This is not the same as the Council of the European Union (above). The European Council does not have formal legislative power but it is an extremely influential institution of the European Union because the members of the council are the heads of member states (prime ministers, presidents, etc). The Treaty of Lisbon says that the Council's obligation is to define the "general political directions and priorities" of the European Union.
Associated Words: Council of European Union (noun), European Union (noun), Prime Minister (person), Treaty (noun).

European Parliament (noun): This organisation is also part of the European Union. It is made up of elected politicians from all the member states in the European Union. They debate and pass laws for the EU that have been proposed by the European Commission.
Associated Words: European Union (noun), To Pass (verb).

European Union Law (noun): This is the general term used in legal English to describe the source of law that comes from the European Parliament, European Commission and Council of the European Union. It mainly consists of treaties, regulations and directives.
Associated Words: Directive (noun), European Parliament (noun), European Commission (noun), Council of the European Union (noun), Regulation (noun), Treaty (noun).

Regulation (noun): This is a type of legislation of the European Union. A regulation is a law that has been passed by the Institutions of the European Union and will have "direct effect" on the member states. This means that it will automatically become law in the member states. The member states do not need to implement the law, because it becomes law in each member state as soon as it comes into force with the European Union.

Associated Words: To Come into Force (collocation), European Union.

Treaty (noun): A treaty is a little bit like a contract and usually used with international law. It is an agreement (commonly between countries or groups of countries) to record in writing all duties and obligations of the parties. Treaties are sometimes called international agreements, conventions, protocols and covenants. One of the most important treaties in relation to the English legal system is the Treaty of Rome, which was agreed in 1959 to establish a common market in Europe. This treaty lead to the establishment of the European Union.

Associated Words: To Breach (verb), Covenant (noun), Duties and Obligations (nouns), European Union (noun).

Note: In 2016 the UK held a referendum in which the majority voted to leave the European Union.

6. PRINCIPLES AND CONCEPTS

Adversarial (adjective): The English legal system is adversarial by nature. This means that there are two sides of advocates who present their case or position to a neutral third party (usually a judge or jury). It is the duty of the advocates to produce evidence to the judge or jury. It is the judge or the jury who then decide which position is the truth in their opinion. The opposite system is called the "inquisitorial" system in which the judge(s) investigate the matter themselves.
Associated Words: Advocate (person), Judge (person), Jury (noun).

Bias (noun): This describes a mental state when someone is subjectively in favour of or against, a particular person, opinion or position. It is generally thought of as a negative word in English as it suggests that someone does not take all relevant facts into consideration, but simply forms their opinion on subjective rather than objective points. To be biased towards someone or something means that you are in favour of it, whilst to be biased against someone or something means that you do not like it or you disagree with it. To use the word as an adjective you would say that a person is "biased" or "unbiased". It is a fundamental principle of the English legal system that the Judiciary is not biased in any way.
Associated Words: To be biased towards (collocation), to be biased against (collocation), Judiciary (noun).

Deed (noun): A deed is a legal document, similar to a contract that has been agreed and signed by all the parties. Certain documents in English law must be signed as a deed, for example, buying land or a house. Another reason for using a deed is if there is an agreement between the parties, but one party is transferring something to another, for example a donation or a gift to charity.
Associated Words: Contract Law (noun), Party (noun).

Due Process (noun): This describes how the legislature, executive and the judiciary should make their decisions. Due process is a phrase that means that all decisions should be made in the correct way, without any unfair influence and obeying the rule of law.

Associated Words: Executive (noun), Judiciary (noun), Legislature (noun), Rule of Law (noun).

Engagement Letter/Client Care Letter (noun): This letter, written by a solicitor to their client, confirms the details of the work that the client has asked the solicitor to do and the agreed terms and conditions. The letter is very important in England and Wales and must include certain pieces of information so that the client has full knowledge of what the solicitor is asked to do (and what they are not asked to do). There are rules for what pieces of information must be in the letter, these include: the type of work to be done for the client, an estimate of cost, the hourly rates of the lawyers working on the matter, complaint procedures, etc.
Associated Words: Matter (noun), Solicitor (person) Terms (noun).

Ethics (noun): These are the rules by which a solicitor or barrister must act and behave in their professional life and outside it. Ethics deals with issues such as acting in good faith, with confidentiality and with no conflicts of interest.
Associated Words: Barrister (person), Good Faith (noun), Solicitor (person).

Fees (noun): This word is used to describe an amount of money charged to a client for a professional service. It is used in a legal context to describe the money that a solicitor, barrister or an expert will charge for their services.
Associated Words: Solicitor (person), Barrister (person).

Formal (adjective): This word, along with its antonym "informal" is used to describe the different styles of expression in both written and spoken language. It is very important in legal English to decide when and how to use either formal language or informal language. Recently, the English legal system has tried to make its language less formal and more "plain" for more people, who are not legally trained, to easily understand legal terms and contracts.

Hearsay (noun): This is the word used for evidence given by a witness about an event that they were told about (but didn't actually witness

themselves). For example, if Tom is a witness and says, "I saw David steal the TV" this is a statement of evidence from Tom that he witnessed the theft. However, if Tom says, "Fred told me that David stole the TV" this evidence is called "hearsay evidence". Hearsay evidence is generally inadmissible in court but there are some exceptions where it is allowed. Inadmissible means not to allow something in court to be heard as evidence.
Associated Words: Court (noun), Evidence (noun), Witness (person).

Human Rights Act 1998 (noun): This very important piece of UK legislation received royal assent in November 1998 and came into force in October 2000. The Human Rights Act 1998 is important because it gives power to the UK courts to hear claims for the infringement of an individual's human rights without having to go to the European Court of Human Rights in Strasbourg. The aim of the Act is to bring the legal effect of the European Convention on Human Rights to the UK courts. It makes it unlawful for any institution of a member state of the European Union to act in a way that is not in agreement with the European Convention on Human Rights. It tries to protect an individual in relation to their fundamental rights to freedom of speech, expression, movement and religion, etc.
Associated Words: To Come into Force (collocation), Court (noun), Legislation (noun), Rights (noun), Royal Assent (noun).

Jurisprudence (noun): This is the word used for the study and theory of law. Generally students will study law at university, but some universities use the term jurisprudence. Those who study jurisprudence wish to obtain understanding of legal systems, the nature of law, legal reasoning and legal institutions.

Legal Aid (noun): This is a general phrase used for money provided to people who do not have enough money for legal representation. This type of financial help is only available in some very special cases and there are many tests used to check if a person should receive Legal Aid. Criminal law and family law cases are areas where Legal Aid is available.
Associated Words: Criminal Law (noun), Family Law (noun).

Legal Entity (noun): This phrase is very common in legal English. A company is a separate legal entity (legal person) and has a separate legal personality from its employees, directors and shareholders.

Judiciary (noun): This word is used to describe the system of courts and judges who interpret the law in England and Wales. Under the separation of powers the judiciary check the legislature and the executive to ensure fairness and justice. The judiciary includes all the judges in all of the courts from the courts of first instance up to the Supreme Court.
Associated Words: Courts of First Instance (noun), Executive (noun), Legislature (noun), Separation of Powers (noun), Supreme Court (noun).

Justice (noun): The English legal system attempts to produce and enforce the law in the interests of justice. Justice means that the decisions of parliament, the courts and the governing authorities are equitable and fair.
Associated Words: Court (noun), Parliament (noun).

Legal Professional Privilege (noun): This is a right that belongs to a lawyer's client which ensures that all communication (letters, etc) that a client has with their lawyer will stay secret and confidential. Usually in litigation proceedings both parties must allow the other party to see all the relevant documents and evidence in the case. However, all communication between a client and their lawyer does not have to be given to the other party because it is privileged and so stays confidential. This privilege belongs to the client, not the lawyer and only the client can choose for a privileged document to be shown to the other party.
Associated Words: Court (noun), Party (noun).

Legalese (noun): this phrase is one of the reasons that lawyers and law students have moved towards a clearer plainer version of legal English. Legalese is the word we use to describe the old, traditional language that is not always easy to understand. Recently there has been a movement to use plainer English so that more people can understand legal terms and concepts.

Legislature (noun): The legislature is one part of the 3 elements that introduce, check and pass laws in the English legal system (the other elements are the executive and the judiciary). The role of the legislature is to debate, vote and pass laws in their jurisdiction. The separation of powers doctrine ensures that these laws are then checked by the executive and the judiciary.

Associated Words: Executive (noun), Judiciary (noun), To Pass (verb), Separation of Powers (noun).

Magic Circle (noun): This is a relatively informal phrase that is used to refer to the 5 leading law firms (and leading barristers' chambers) which have their main office in the United Kingdom. The top 5 law firms are generally decided by the amount of profit they make, but generally it is an informal way of referring to the largest and most prestigious law firms.

Magna Carta (noun): The Magna Carta (Latin for "great charter") is one of the most important documents in the English legal system's history. It was written in 1215 and it is one of only a few documents to state something similar to a constitutional right for the individual (the English legal system does not have a written constitution). Only 3 clauses of the Magna Carta are still in force, including clause 29 which states that each person has the right to due process and a fair trial.

Associated Words: Due Process (noun), Right (noun).

Matter (noun): this term is very commonly used to describe a case, transaction or an issue.

No Win No Fee (collocation): This phrase is used to describe the situation where a law firm agrees to represent a client and that the client will only have to pay a fee to the lawyer if the client wins the case (or if the claim is settled). These types of fee agreement are not always possible, but they are common in personal injury claims.

Associated Word: Fee (noun).

Oath (noun): To make an oath means to promise something. It is a very common phrase in legal English as it is used with stating that something is true to the best of your knowledge. The most common example of someone making an oath would be when witnesses give evidence in court. Before a witness gives evidence, they will explain to the court that they promise to tell the truth. This is called making an oath to the court. The collocation "to swear an oath" is also commonly heard and has the same meaning.

Associated Words: To Swear an Oath (collocation), Court (noun), Evidence (noun).

Obligation (noun): An obligation is something that a person must do. An obligation can be legal or moral but within the English legal system it is common to see the words "duties and obligations" especially in commercial contracts. This means that the parties to the contract must do (or must not do) whatever is written in this section of the contract. In legal English the phrase "to fulfil an obligation" is very common. To fulfil an obligation means to complete it.

Associated Words: Contract Law (noun), Party (noun).

Precedent – meaning 2 of 2 (noun): In this second context the word precedent refers to a template or a standard document. This template can then be used with information from the client to create a specific version with the client's information. It is common for large law firms to have precedent banks or precedent libraries where they keep a large collection of precedent documents so that lawyers will not have to produce documents from a blank page. It is one of the most common tools for lawyers to use and there are thousands of different precedents for all of the different areas of law.

Procedure (noun): This means that there are set ways in which things must be done. It refers to keeping order and stability in the way the laws are passed and the cases are heard. In the English legal system, especially the judiciary, one of the most important doctrines is procedure. Passing laws in parliament, civil claims and criminal cases must all follow set procedures. Each part of the system will have its own procedure and it is very important for lawyers and courts to follow them. One of the most important documents in the English legal system is the Civil Procedure Rules, which explains the rules and regulations that must be followed for all civil claims.

Associated Words: Civil Law (noun), Judiciary (noun), Parliament (noun).

Rule of Law (noun): The rule of law is a complicated subject both for lawyers and non-lawyers. In the English legal system, the rule of law can be explained in 3 main parts (there are many other parts too). First, the law making process must be clear. This means that the process for making the laws of the country must be understandable and must follow a clear process. The Government must be legal itself and should not be able to pass whatever laws it wants. Second, the law must be equal and the same for everybody. Third, the law is supreme and is the highest point of guidance for all. Of course, the rule of law is much wider than these three points and it is a very large subject of study. Other principles of the rule of law include; independence of the judiciary, judicial review of the implementation of laws and rules and an individual's access to the courts
Associated Words: Court (noun), Government (noun), Judiciary (noun).

Rights (noun): This is the general legal English term for legal, social, moral or ethical principles or freedoms that a person has (or feels they should have). Rights are seen to be essential for society and culture to exist freely.

Source of Law (noun): This phrase means where the law began or originated. In the English legal system there are a number of sources. The two most important sources of law are precedents in common law and legislation of parliament.
Associated Words: Legislation (noun), Parliament (noun), Precedent (noun).

Separation of Powers (noun): This is a model of government where the most important law and policy-making authorities are kept independent of each other. The reason for this is to make sure that the laws are fair and equal. In the English legal system the three authorities are the legislature (parliament), the executive (the cabinet and government departments) and the judiciary (the courts). In practice the model is far more complicated than this but generally these three authorities should be kept independent of each other under the principle of the separation of powers.
Associated Words: Cabinet (noun), Court (noun), Executive (noun), Government (noun), Judiciary (noun), Legislature (noun), Parliament (noun).

Term – meaning 1 of 2 (noun): In one context this word means duration. For example, you will regularly hear lawyers discussing the "term" of the contract. In this context they are discussing the duration, or for how much time the contract is be valid.

Term – meaning 2 of 2 (noun): In another legal English context, the word "term" means a word or phrase. For example, "the legal term for the verb to sue is to issue proceedings".

Terms (noun): This word means a clause or a provision in a contract or agreement. It is one of the most common words used in relation to contract law and it is often used with the phrase "terms and conditions".

Ultra Vires (noun): This Latin phrase, which translates as "beyond the power", is an important phrase in the English legal system. It is used in administrative law and was developed to make sure that the decisions made by government authorities (and other positions of power) were made correctly and within their given power. If a decision is found to be ultra vires by the court, then it is possible for the court to find that the decision is unlawful.
Associated Words: Administrative Law (noun), Government (noun).

Vicarious Liability (noun): This is an important doctrine of the law of tort. Vicarious liability means that an employer is automatically liable for the wrong doing (torts) of their employees. For example, if a pizza deliveryman causes a road accident while delivering pizzas, both the pizza deliveryman and the pizza company he works for will be liable.
Associated Words: Tort Law (noun).

Unwritten Constitution (noun): The English legal system does not have one written document that can be called its constitution. Rather, there are many documents that are used to piece together a set of moral, ethical and fundamental rights that produce an unwritten constitution. For instance, the Magna Carta (see above) was and still is a document that states certain fundamental rights and principles. The doctrine of precedent has developed a number of other rights and principles that can be used to establish the basic fundamental rights of England and Wales. More recently the Human Rights Act 1998 added to these fundamental rights, but as a whole, England and Wales has an unwritten constitution.

Associated Words: Human Rights Act (noun), Magna Carta (noun), Precedent (noun), Rights (noun).

To Waive (verb): This verb means that you do not want to have a right or claim that you previously had before. It is commonly used in relation to the right of privilege (see above). For example, if Mr White writes a letter to his solicitor then this letter has legal professional privilege and he does not have to show this letter to other lawyers or the court in legal proceedings. However, there may be some important information in that letter that Mr White wants the court to see. Mr White can "waive" his right to legal professional privilege here and show the letter to the court.

Associated Words: Waived (past simple), Waived (3rd form), Court (noun), Legal Professional Privilege (noun), Solicitor (person).

Without Prejudice (noun): If a letter from a lawyer has the words "Without Prejudice" written as a heading then it means that the letter should not be shown to the court or the judge. Without prejudice correspondence is a safe way of communicating with other parties with the comfort that the letter is confidential from the court. It is generally used in settlement negotiations in disputes as it allows the lawyers to be more open knowing that the court will not see the letter.

Associated Words: Court (noun), Judge (noun).

7. GLOSSARY

People in Law:

To Act for/To Act on Behalf of
To Advise
Attorney
Attorney General
Bar Council
Barrister
Bench
District Judge
To Draft
Immunity
Indemnity Insurance
In-House
Inns of Court
Judge
Jury
The Law Society
Layperson
Member of Parliament
Monarch
Notary Public
Ombudsman
Partnership
Peer
To Practise
Prime Minister
To Qualify
Queen's Counsel
Sole Practitioner
Solicitor
To Specialise
Training Contract

To Undertake

Areas of Law:

Administrative Law
Banking and Finance
Bankruptcy
Civil Law
Criminal Law
To Commit
Common Law
Company Law
Contentious
Contract Law
Conveyancing
Defamation
Divorce
Employment Law
Family Law
Insolvency Law
Intellectual Property Law
Immigration Law
To Inherit
Landlord and Tenant Law
Libel
Mergers and Acquisitions
Non-Contentious
Real Estate Law
Slander
Tax Law
Tort Law/The Law of Tort
Trust Law/The Law of Trusts
Wills

The Courts:

Admiralty Court
Advocacy
To Appeal
Appellate Court
To Bind
Chancery Division
Court
Commercial Court
County Court
Court of Appeal
Court of First Instance
To Dissent
To Distinguish
Family Division
High Court of Justice
To Hear
To Impose
Jurisdiction
Judgment
Law Reports
Obiter Dictum
To Overrule
Precedent – meaning 1 of 2
Party
To Prove
Queen's Bench Division
Ratio Decidendi
To Resolve
The Royal Courts of Justice
To Reverse
Supreme Court
To Sue
Technology and Construction Court
Tribunal

To Uphold Verdict
To Witness

Parliament:

Act of Parliament
To Ban
Bill
By-Election
By-Law
Cabinet
Constitutional Monarchy
To Come Into Force
Delegated Legislation
Devolution
Election
General Election
Government
Green Paper
House of Commons
House of Lords
Houses of Parliament
Hansard
Home Office
Hung Parliament
To Implement
Legislation
Member of Parliament
Monarch
Parliament
To Pass
Peer
To Repeal
Royal Assent
Secondary Legislation
Statute

Statutory Instrument

White Paper

European Law:

Council of the European Union

Directive

European Commission

European Court of Human Rights

European Court of Justice

European Council

European Parliament

European Union Law

Regulation

Treaty

Principles and Concepts:

Adversarial

Bias

Deed

Due Process

Engagement Letter/Client Care Letter

Ethics

Fees

Formal

Hearsay

Human Rights Act 1998

Jurisprudence

Legal Aid

Legal Entity

Judiciary

Justice

Legal Professional Privilege

Legalese

Legislature

Magic Circle

Magna Carta

Matter

No Win No Fee

Oath

Obligation

Precedent – meaning 2 of 2

Procedure

Rule of Law

Rights

Source of Law

Separation of Powers

Term – meaning 1 of 2

Term – meaning 2 of 2

Terms

Ultra Vires

Vicarious Liability

Unwritten Constitution

To Waive

Without Prejudice

THE ENGLISH LEGAL SYSTEM

8. EXERCISES

TRUE OR FALSE

Decide if these sentences are true or false (answers are at the back of the book):

1. Hearsay evidence is generally inadmissible in English courts.

2. The highest court in the English legal system is the Court of Appeal.

3. The idea of the separation of powers is that the legislature, executive and the judiciary must be kept independent of each other.

4. When a bill receives royal assent from the monarch, the phrase to come into force is used because the law has legal effect from the date the bill was signed.

5. The UK Government consists of the House of Commons and the House of Lords.

6. The verb to repeal means that the passing of a bill has been delayed by the House of Lords.

7. The word precedent means template or standard document. It does not have any other meaning in legal English.

8. In legal English, judges can collectively be referred to as the bench.

9. Intellectual property law deals with matters such as copyright, trademarks and patents.

10. An oath is a promise by a solicitor to do something, or cause something to be done. If they fail to do this, they may be found to be in breach of their professional code of conduct.

11. Under English law, a company is a separate legal entity from its shareholders and directors.

12. If a court is in the correct location and has authority to hear and decide a case, the court has jurisdiction to hear to the case.

13. If a letter from a lawyer to another lawyer is marked "Without Prejudice", the letter is not allowed to be shown to the court.

14. The ratio decidendi is the part of the judgment that explains the history, factual background and the general arguments in a case.

15. A by-law is a law that can be delegated to local authorities in order for laws to be created easily without the need for Parliament to debate them.

16. To sue is the formal way of saying to go to court or to start a claim at court.

17. Tort law is very complicated but the simplest way to explain it is to say that it deals with civil wrongs.

18. An ultra vires decision made by a government department means that the department has authority to make that decision.

19. The English legal system is adversarial in nature. This means that the judges' role is to listen to advocates from all sides of the case and to decide the verdict based on the evidence shown to them.

20. The three main parts of the English legal system are the judiciary, executive and the legislature.

VOCABULARY GAP FILL

Complete the sentences with the missing word or phrase (answers are at the back of the book):

1. The communication of legal advice between a lawyer and their client does not have to be shown to other lawyers or the court during legal proceedings because the communication has _____ _____ _____.

2. The courts and judges together are called the _____. They are one of the three important parts of the separation of powers.

3. The verbs "to reverse" or "to _____" are very similar in meaning. They both mean that a higher court disagrees with the lower court's decision and change the original verdict.

4. The _____ _____ is a Latin phrase and means the part of the judgment that forms the binding precedent.

5. The transfer, registration and the buying and selling of houses is more commonly known as _____.

6. One of the most important letters that a lawyer will write is at the start of the relationship with the client. It informs the client of the type of work that will be done, the fee and the terms and conditions of the service. This letter is called the _____letter or the _____ _____ letter.

7. A lawyer in England and Wales who wears a horsehair wig and black gown is called a _____.

8. The legal English word for a person who is not a lawyer or is not legally qualified is a _____.

9. To _____ _____ _____ is a common phrase that means that a law is now in existence.

10. In the UK a lawyer is either a barrister or a solicitor. In the USA they are generally called _____.

11. Before an act becomes law, it is called a _____.

12. The system of _____ _____ uses binding precedents from higher courts to establish legal principles which must be followed by lower courts.

13. A _____ is a legal document that must be signed by all parties. It is a type of contract and is commonly used for transfers of land or property.

14. One of the most important pieces of legislation in recent years is the _____ _____ _____. This statute is designed to protect an individual's freedom and other fundamental rights.

15. A lawyer who practises _____ _____ will usually have to deal with companies who are unable to pay their debts and may have to begin legal proceedings to close the company.

16. The name of the organisation in England and Wales who represent solicitors is called _____ _____ _____.

17. The name of the (usually) long report given by a judge at the end of the case explaining their decision is called the _____.

18. The law must be clear and made using a fair process. It must be understandable, it must be equal for everyone and everyone must follow it. These principles are part of the doctrine called _____ _____ _____ _____.

19. If an employee commits a tort while working for their employer, the employer could also be _____ _____.

20. The European Parliament, European Commission and Council of the European Union responsible for proposing, drafting and implementing _____ _____ law.

PREPOSITION GAP FILL

Complete the sentences using the correct preposition (answers are at the back of the book):

1. My oldest client came to me in 1995. I have acted _____ him in relation to his divorce, the sale of his business and drafting his last will and testament.

2. A friend of mine has a problem with her company. Some of her customers have not paid their invoices to her. She would like me to act _____ behalf of the company to collect the unpaid invoices.

3. I have a busy day tomorrow. I have a client meeting at 10am and have to be _____ court at 2pm for a hearing regarding my client's personal injury claim.

4. When the courts look at precedents from previous cases they may decide that the cases are relevant and so will consider them further. Alternatively, they may distinguish them _____ the present case because they are not relevant or similar enough.

5. It is a lifetime ambition for some people to be elected _____ a Member of Parliament.

6. Law is a difficult subject and so it takes a long time and lots of effort to study _____ an exam.

7. In criminal law, the court will impose a prison sentence _____ a defendant if the crime is serious enough.

8. I loved my corporate seat during my training contract and now I'm a qualified solicitor and work _____ the M&A department.

9. Many law graduates have ambitions of becoming a lawyer for one of the bigger law firms. Accordingly, they will try to work _____ a magic circle firm.

10. The judge disagreed with the defendant's arguments and found _____ favour of the claimant.

11. People who are in positions of responsibility, for example, solicitors and directors of companies have a duty to act _____ good faith when providing their services.

12. After working as a barrister for 23 years, Mark Robinson sat _____ a judge in the High Court before retiring.

13. The parties finally agreed that the term _____ the contract will be 5 years.

14. In the tort of negligence, a person owes a duty _____ care to other people in some situations.

15. One of the unique principles of the English legal system is trial _____ jury. The principle means that you are judged by your colleagues.

16. David successfully passed his exams to become a barrister. He can now be called _____ the Bar.

17. In some countries, Members of Parliament are immune _____ prosecution for some crimes.

18. In the English legal system, if a precedent is relevant to a present case, then that precedent is binding _____ the lower courts to follow the precedent.

19. Once a bill has been passed by the Houses of Parliament and has received royal assent, it becomes an act. Usually the act will then come _____ force, but sometimes this date is delayed.

20. Henry was very nervous because at 3pm he had to appear _____ court for the first time as a barrister.

COLLOCATION GAP FILL

Complete the sentences using the correct collocation (answers are at the back of the book):

1. A _____ to a case is an individual or organisation who has an interest in the case or claim. Usually they are in the form of a claimant and a defendant.

2. Due to the high number of claims, the court cannot _____ the case until next month. All parties will be informed of the date.

3. After 3 hours, the judge returned to the courtroom and _____ judgment in favour of the claimant.

4. After hearing evidence from both parties, I have decided to _____ the appeal. The case will be heard again in the Court of Appeal next year.

5. There are many ways to _____ a business. Private limited companies, partnerships or sole traders are three options.

6. My neighbour told me that he is insolvent. He cannot pay his debts but he will not _____ bankrupt until the court has declared this.

7. A member of the House of Lords is not allowed to _____ in the House of Commons.

8. It is common for qualified lawyers to work for a company or an organisation (not a law firm). These lawyers are called _____ _____ lawyers.

9. Many cases are brought in the wrong _____. This means that the court does not have authority to hear the case.

10. The government want to _____ a new law to give the police more powers.

11. Helen was _____ to the Bar in 1996. She is an expert in intellectual property law.

12. In a commercial contract there will be many _____ and conditions which both parties need to read carefully.

13. Before giving evidence in court a witness will have to _____ an oath that they will tell the truth.

14. It is very important to _____ procedure in the English legal system. An example of this is the Civil Procedure Rules.

15. The Human Rights Act says that I _____ the right to the freedom of speech.

16. Before a bill becomes an act it must _____ royal assent. This is when the monarch signs the bill.

17. A car driver was driving his car too fast and crashed into my car. I want to _____ him __ ____ negligent driving and I want compensation for my losses.

18. If a solicitor promises to the court that they will do something or cause something to be done, it is said that they _____ an undertaking to the court.

19. The final hearing has finished, when will the judge _____ down judgment?

20. Some defamation cases are conducted by lawyers on a "no win no _____" basis.

REPLACE THE INCORRECT WORD

Replace the *incorrect* word with the correct one (answers are at the back of the book):

1. In some countries the monarchy and members of parliament are immune *of* [_____] prosecution for some crimes.

2. All barristers and solicitors must have indemnity insurance. This means that if they *do* [_____] a mistake, the losses are paid by an insurance company.

3. There are two main types of law in England and Wales. One type is criminal law and the other type is *common* [_____] law.

4. The skill of speaking in court is known as *hearing* [_____].

5. Slander and libel are types of *family* [_____] law.

6. The form of business usually used by law firms is called a *private limited company* [_____].

7. The largest law firms in the UK are sometimes referred to as the *golden* [_____] circle firms.

8. The criminal told the police that he didn't *do* [_____] the crime.

9. Members of the House of Lords can be referred to as Lords or Ladies. Together they can also be referred to as *MPs* [_____].

10. One of the most important doctrines in the English legal system is the system of *obiter dictum* [_____ _____]. This is when the lower courts must follow the decisions of the higher courts.

11. The twelve laypeople who sit in court and decide the verdict in a case are called the *bench* [_____].

12. When a person dies the document that states which person inherits the assets is called a *deed* [_____].

13. A King or Queen is also known as a *peer* [_____].

14. The system of binding precedents is central to the concept of _civil_ [_____] law.

15. The main European Union laws are called _acts, statutes and bills_ [_____, _____ and _____]

16. Lawyers can _do_ [_____] many different areas or specialisations, but usually they specialise soon after qualifying.

17. Politicians are more formally known as members of _government_ [_____].

18. The part of the judgment that forms the binding precedent is called the _ultra vires_ [_____ _____]

19. In legal English it is said that the lower courts are _held_ [_____] by the decisions of the higher courts.

20. The European _Court of Justice_ [_____} is an organisation based in Brussels, Belgium. It is the organisation that proposes what laws are needed in the European Union.

9. ANSWERS

True or False:

1. True

2. False

3. True

4. False

5. False

6. False

7. False

8. True

9. True

10. False

11. True

12. True

13. True

14. False

15. True

16. False

17. True

18. False

19. True

20. True

Vocabulary Gap Fill:

1. legal professional privilege

2. judiciary

3. overrule

4. ratio decidendi

5. conveyancing

6. engagement letter/client care letter

7. barrister

8. layperson

9. come into force

10. attorneys

11. bill

12. common law

13. deed

14. Human Rights Act

15. insolvency law

16. The Law Society

17. judgment

18. the rule of law

19. vicariously liable

20. European Union law

Prepositions Gap Fill:

1. for

2. on

3. in/at

4. from

5. as

6. for

7. on

8. in

9. for

10. in

11. in

12. as

13. of

14. of

15. by

16. to, as

17. from

18. on

19. into

20. in

Collocations Gap Fill:

1. party

2. hear

3. gave/found

4. allow

5. form

6. go

7. sit

8. in-house

9. jurisdiction

10. pass

11. called

12. terms

13. swear/give

14. follow

15. have

16. receive

17. sue, for

18. give

19. hand

20. fee

Replace the Incorrect Word

1. ~~of~~, from

2. ~~do~~, make

3. ~~common~~, civil

4. ~~hearing~~, advocacy

5. ~~family law~~, defamation

6. ~~private limited company~~, partnership

7. ~~golden~~, magic

8. ~~do~~, commit

9. ~~MPs~~, peers

10. ~~obiter dictum~~, binding precedents/common law

11. ~~bench~~, jury

12. ~~deed~~, will

13. ~~peer~~, monarch

14. ~~civil~~, common

15. ~~acts, statutes and bills~~, treaties, regulations and directives

16. ~~do~~, practise

17. ~~government~~, parliament

18. ~~ultra vires~~, ratio decidendi

19. ~~held~~, bound

20. ~~Court of Justice~~, Commission

B. DRAFTING COMMERCIAL CONTRACTS

1. TYPES OF CONTRACTS

Agency Agreement (noun): An agency agreement is an arrangement between two parties where one party (the "principal") asks another party (the "agent") to represent them and create contractual legal relationships with a third party. This means that the agent has authority to make decisions for the principal and will negotiate directly with the third party. Agency agreements are very common and are used for marketing, distribution, customer support and many other types of contracts. For example, Company A (the principal) manufactures cars in Japan. Company A authorises company B (the agent) to advertise the car in Brazil. Company B negotiates and contracts with television company C (the third party) to show a number of TV advertisements for the car in Brazil. In this example, there will be an agency agreement between company A and company B for company B to represent company A in the contract negotiations with company C.
Associated Words: Agent (noun), Distribution (Noun), Marketing (noun), Principal (noun), Third Party (noun).

Consumer Credit Agreement (noun): This is a contract where a third party (usually a bank) agrees to finance the purchase of the goods or services. This contract is separate from the contract between the buyer and seller.
Associated Words: Goods (noun), To Purchase (verb), Third Party (noun).

Distance Selling (noun): A distance selling contract is a contract, which is performed without the parties meeting face to face. Examples of distance selling contracts are internet sales, catalogue sales, sales via telephone, sales by email and sales by fax. There are specific regulations for these types of contracts to ensure that the consumer is given the same rights and protection as a consumer would if they entered the contract face to face with the seller.
Associated Words: Consumer (noun), Seller (noun), Rights (noun).

Distribution Agreement (noun): A distribution agreement is a contract between a manufacturer of goods and a third party. The third party is responsible for marketing and distributing the goods. Usually, under a distribution agreement, the third party will market and sell the goods using their own name. One important difference between a distribution agreement and an agency agreement is that under a distribution agreement title and ownership of the goods will usually pass to the third party (and so does the risk). Under an agency agreement the title and ownership of the goods remains with the manufacturer until the goods are sold to the final buyer.

Associated Words: Agency Agreement (noun), Marketing (noun), Risk (noun), Third Party (noun), Title to Goods (noun).

E-commerce (noun): This is a general term for trading and commercial contracts entered into over the internet. There are special considerations when entering into such contracts such as data protection and secure payment methods.

Associated Words: Data Protection (noun), To Enter Into (phrasal verb).

Franchise (noun): This is a type of agreement where a company (A) grants a licence to another company (B) to sell, manufacture or distribute company A's products. Company B will usually use company A's method, trademarks and technology and will be paid a royalty or commission from the profit. For example, company A is a well-known fast-food restaurant chain and wants to expand its network of restaurants. They can enter into franchise agreements with other independent companies who will run the restaurants (or "franchises") in exactly the same way as the original restaurants, using all the same methods and trademarks. This agreement is very useful for well-known brands with well-established trademarks and reputations that wish to expand their business.

Associated Words: Commission (noun), To Grant (verb), Licence (noun), Profit (noun), Trademark (noun).

To Hire (verb): This verb means paying money to borrow something from someone or to use a product or service temporarily. To hire is commonly used in relation to hiring goods such as cars, bicycles, boats, etc. A hire-purchase agreement is a contract where the goods or services for hire become permanently owned by the buyer after all payments have been made to the seller.

Associated Words: Hire Agreement (noun), Hire Purchase Agreement

(noun).

Hire Agreement (noun): This is a contract between a person (the "Hirer") who pays to use a product or service for a period of time. This type of contract is used between a hirer and an owner when the owner loans its goods to the hirer for use without an option to purchase them.
Associated Words: To Hire (verb), Hirer (noun), To Loan (verb), To Purchase (verb).

Hire-Purchase Agreements (noun): This agreement is similar to a hire agreement but the hirer has the option to purchase the goods after a period of time, or after a certain amount of the loan has been re-paid.
Associated Words: To Hire (verb), To Loan (verb), Option (noun), To Purchase (verb).

Insurance (noun): An insurance agreement is an agreement between an insurance company (the "insurer") and a customer (the "insured"). The insured pays a premium, for example every month, so that in the future the insurer will compensate the insured for any loss suffered which is covered by the insurance agreement. There are many difference types of insurance agreement and each type has very specific conditions that the insured must meet in order for the insurer to compensate the loss suffered. The terms of the agreement are set out in a long document called an insurance policy.
Associated Words: To Insure (verb), Insured (noun), Insurer (noun), To Compensate (verb), Conditions (noun), Loss (noun), To Set Out (verb), To Suffer (verb).

Lease (noun): This is a very popular type of agreement that permits a party to use property, land, vehicles or a piece of equipment for a period of time. Under a lease agreement ownership and legal title remains with the owner.
Associated Word: Title (noun).

To License (verb): This verb means to give permission to use something for a period of time. A person who gives permission or a license is called a "licensor" and the receiver is called a "licensee". A common example of the verb would be in intellectual property law where copyright or patents are sometimes licensed between licensors and licensees. The contract is referred to as a Licence Agreement. An important aspect of a licence agreement is that legal title will remain with the licensor. In British English the noun of the verb is spelt "licence", while in American English is it spelt "license".

Associated Words: Licence (British English noun), License (American English noun), Licensee (noun), Licensor (noun).

Loan Agreement (noun): This is a very common commercial contract between a creditor (for example, a bank) and a debtor. A loan agreement is a contract where the debtor will borrow money from the creditor and agrees to pay the money back, usually in instalments, plus interest for an agreed period of time.

Associated Words: To Loan (verb), To Borrow (verb), Creditor (noun), Debtor (noun), Instalments (noun), Interest (noun).

Marketing (noun): This is an agreement for one party to conduct the promotion and advertising of goods or services for the manufacturer or seller.

Associated Word: Goods (noun).

Outsourcing (noun): To outsource means to transfer the duties and obligations of delivering a service to an external provider. This external provider will then provide the service. Common outsourcing agreements used by businesses are for IT services, telephone call centres and basic office administration. For example, it is common for global banks to outsource their telephone banking services to countries with lower costs. Outsourcing agreements are more complex than straightforward contracts for the supply of goods or services as they often involve the transfer of people, assets and contracts.

Associated Words: To Outsource (verb), Outsourced (adjective), Assets (noun), Duties and Obligations (collocation), Supply of Goods (collocation), Supply of Services (noun).

Sale of Goods (noun): This agreement governs the common contract between a buyer and seller. Goods is a general word for products or things for sale. Usually, these contracts will include conditions on price, term, termination, title, description, quality, quantity, exclusivity and dispute resolution.

Associated Words: Goods (noun), Conditions (noun), Exclusivity (noun), Quality (noun), Quantity (noun), Term (noun), Termination (noun), Title (noun).

Subrogation (noun): This is when a third party is given the rights or remedies of a claimant against a defendant. For example, Mr Smith takes out car insurance with LE Insurance Co Ltd. Mr Grim negligently crashes his car into Mr Smith's car causing £1,000 worth of damage. Mr Smith makes a claim with his insurance company to pay for the damage. Mr Smith also wants to issue a claim against Mr Grim for the £1,000. However, under the doctrine of subrogation, this right has been taken from Mr Smith by LE Insurance. LE Insurance may claim the £1,000 from Mr Grim but Mr Smith cannot. If Mr Smith also made this claim he would receive £1,000 from LE insurance and £1,000 from Mr Grim. This means that Mr Smith would receive compensation for the same loss twice (£2,000 in total). This is classed as unjust enrichment and is stopped by the doctrine of subrogation. Mr Smith may still have a claim against Mr Grim for any personal injury suffered. This is a different claim and so he would be free to issue a separate claim for it because this right was not subrogated to LE Insurance.
Associated Words: To Subrogate (verb), To Issue a Claim (collocation), Third Party (noun), Unjust Enrichment (noun).

Supply of Services (collocation): This is an agreement between one or more parties to provide a service in exchange for payment. Most agreements for a provision of a service are done in short form, however if the agreement is for a long term service then a more extensive agreement is required. Such an agreement needs to include terms and conditions for price, inflation, third party costs, employment and transport costs, customer changes to the service, development and improvement costs, term, termination, performance levels (the customer may want to set performance levels for the supplier using key performance indicators (KPIs), force majeure, remedies, quality of the services to be provided, exclusivity and dispute resolution.
Associated Words: Dispute Resolution (noun), Exclusivity (noun), Force Majeure (noun), Inflation (noun), Key Performance Indicators (noun), Price (noun), Term (noun), Termination (noun), Terms and Conditions (collocation), Third Party (noun).

2. HOW IS A CONTRACT CREATED?

To Accept (verb): This verb is common in commercial contract law as it means that a party agrees to the terms and conditions of an agreement or contract is offered to them. It is the unconditional acceptance of the offer (without changing any of the terms) that forms the basis of a contract in law. There are other legal factors that must also be satisfied, for instance consideration, intention and authority to contract.

Associated Words: Accepted (past simple), Accepted (3rd form), Acceptance (noun), Authority to Contract (collocation), Consideration (noun), Party (noun), Terms and Conditions (collocation), (adjective).

To Affirm (verb): This verb means to say yes, to confirm or to answer in a positive way. In relation to commercial contracts, to affirm a contract means to confirm it is valid or enforceable.

Associated Words: To Enforce (verb), Valid (adjective).

To Amend (verb): This means to change. In legal English when a contract or document is changed or altered, the correct verb to use is to amend.

Authority to Contract (collocation): A party must have authority to enter into a legally binding contract. This means that they must have the right to sign the contract, either for themselves or for an organisation. It is very important that an individual has authority to contract because if they do not, the contract may not be legally binding. For example, for a company to enter into a contract, it will be usually signed by one (or two) of the company directors. These directors must have the company's permission to sign contracts on behalf of the company. If they have the company's permission, then the directors have authority to contract.

Associated Words: To Bind (verb), To Enter into a Contract (collocation).

To Breach (verb): This is a very important word in legal English. It means that someone has broken an agreement or has not done something that they should have done. It is commonly used in commercial contracts, for example "breach of terms and conditions" or "breach of obligations".

Associated Words: Breached (past simple), Breached (3rd form), Breach (noun), Obligations (noun), Terms and Conditions (collocations).

Capacity to Contract (collocation): This phrase means that a party who signs a contract, intended to sign it and understands the terms and conditions that are stated in it. However, if a party does not have capacity to contract then it is not legally binding on that party. Common examples of parties who do not have capacity to contract are minors (children) and people who are mentally impaired or disabled. It is interesting to note that a contract that is in a different language to the party who signs it (and doesn't understand it) may still be legally bound by the contract.
Associated Words: To Bind (verb), Party (noun).

To Consent (verb): This means to allow or to permit something to be done or to happen.

Consideration (noun): This is necessary to form a legally binding contract and for a legal contract to be enforceable, it must have consideration. Consideration means that a transaction must take place and that both parties must receive something. In legal English, the phrase used is that consideration must be reciprocal. This means that consideration must travel both ways. The easiest example to use is the sale of goods. For example, Company X sells 10 television sets to Company Z for 5000 Euros. The consideration moving from Company X to Company Z is the 10 televisions. The consideration moving the other way is the 5000 Euros. In this transaction the consideration is reciprocal and has travelled both ways. This is called good consideration.
Associated Words: To Bind (verb), To Enforce (verb), Goods (noun).

Damages (noun): This is the legal English word for compensation or money paid by the liable party to the successful party. Please note that this noun is already plural and does not have a singular form. The noun "damage" means broken and is not a legal English term. Accordingly, the two words, damage and damages are completely different and should not be confused. Damages is a very important concept of civil litigation and this is the most common remedy awarded by the courts.

Associated Words: Liable (noun), Party (noun), Remedy (noun).

To Dispute (verb): This verb means to argue about something or to question something. It is used in legal English both as a verb and as a noun. The noun "dispute" is a situation when two or more people disagree about something. Civil litigation claims are also commonly called disputes.
Associated Words: Disputed (past simple), Disputed (3rd form), Dispute (noun), Disputed (adjective).

Duress (noun): The term "under duress" means that a person is being forced to do something that they do not want to do. It is similar in meaning to being put under pressure. In a legal English context it means that someone is forcing a party to sign or execute a contract that they do not want to sign. A party may be able to argue that a contract is not valid if they signed it "under duress". A similar phrase that is sometimes used is "undue influence".
Associated Words: Under Duress (collocation), To Execute (verb), Party (noun), Valid (noun).

To Enforce (verb): This means that the contract (or a clause in the contract) is legal and binding and can used or relied on in a court of law.
Associated Words: Enforced (past simple), Enforced (3rd form), Enforceable (adjective), To Bind (verb), To Rely On (phrasal verb).

To Enter Into (phrasal verb): This verb is used in relation to negotiating or signing a contract. The phrase "to enter into negotiations" and "to enter into an agreement" are commonly used to describe the act of agreeing to negotiate or agreeing to contract with another party. For example, it is usual to hear sentences such as *"The contact was entered into on 6th September 2013"*.
Associated Words: Entered Into (past simple), Entered Into (3rd form), To Negotiate (verb).

To Expire (verb): This verb is used in legal English when a contract or time period ends. The context in which it is used is when such a contract or time period finishes naturally or without enforcement. The verb "to terminate" is also used in relation to the end of a contract.
Associated Words: Expired (past simple), Expired (3rd form), Expired

(adjective), Expiry (noun), Expiration (noun), Termination (noun).

Frustration (noun): This means that a contract will be discharged because an event or situation caused the main duties and obligations of the contract to be impossible to be fulfiled. Examples of frustration are when it is impossible to fulfil obligations, that it is illegal to fulfil obligations or that the good or service is unavailable and so cannot be provided. For example, Mr Thomas hires a theatre to perform a music concert. Two days before the concert there is a storm and the theatre is flooded with water. It is impossible to perform the contract because of the doctrine of frustration.
Associated Words: To Frustrate (verb), To Discharge (verb), Duties and Obligations (collocation), To Fulfil (verb), To Hire (verb).

Heads of Terms (noun): This is a document that sets out the basic terms of a contract. It is commonly used for pre-contractual negotiations and to detail the terms that the parties think are the most important. Heads of Terms commonly include the main duties and obligations, for instance, applicable law, price, description, warranties, indemnities, exclusivity, dispute resolution and confidentiality. Heads of Terms are commonly used as a starting point for a first draft of a commercial contract.
Associated Words: Applicable Law (noun), Confidentiality (noun), Description (noun), Duties and Obligations (noun), Exclusivity (noun), Indemnity (noun), To Negotiate (verb), Party (noun), Pre-Contractual (noun), Price (noun), To Set Out (phrasal verb), Warranty (noun).

Injunction (noun): This is a type of remedy available from the court. An injunction is an order from the court that states that a party must do something or stop from doing something. A party who does not follow or obey an injunction can be liable in both criminal and civil law and can face serious penalties if they do not comply with the injunction.
Associated Word: Remedy (noun).

Intention (noun): This means that a party wants to contract with another party and enters into a contract knowing that they are entering into a legally binding situation. In legal English it is very important that all parties to the contract have the intention to contract.

Associated Words: To Intend (verb), Intended (past simple), Intended (3rd form), To Bind (verb), To Contract (verb), To Enter Into (collocation), Party (noun).

To Let (verb): This verb means that the owner of property, land, vehicles or pieces of equipment permits the hirer to use it for a period of time. It is important to understand the difference between the verb to rent and to let. For example, the landlord lets the property to the tenant. The tenant rents the property from the landlord.
Associated Words: Let (past simple), Let (3rd form), Landlord (noun), To Rent (verb), Tenant (noun).

Liquidated Damages (verb): Some contracts will state how much a party must pay if they are in breach of contract. This is called liquidated damages. In legal English there is a difference between liquidated damages and a penalty clause. Penalty clauses are not enforceable under English law and so for a liquidated damages clause to be valid the amount of the damages must be a genuine pre-estimate of loss.
Associated Words: Unliquidated Damages (noun), To Breach (verb), Damages (noun), To Enforce (verb), Loss (noun), Penalty Clause (noun), Valid (adjective).

Mitigation of Loss (collocation): This is a concept in common law that means that a person who has suffered loss must take reasonable action to stop or reduce any further loss or damage. If the defendant can establish in court that the claimant did not mitigate their loss, the court may reduce the award for damages to the claimant.
Associated Words: To Mitigate (verb), Damages (noun).

To Negotiate (verb): This verb means for two or more parties to discuss each party's positions with a view to agreeing a settlement, agreement or a contract. It is one of the most common verbs used in legal English as it is applied in all areas of law. Specifically, commercial contracts will always be negotiated between the parties and their legal representatives to agree a suitable compromise.
Associated Words: Negotiated (past simple), Negotiated (3rd form),

Negotiation (noun), Compromise (noun), Party (noun), Settlement (noun).

To Offer (verb): This verb is the first step to enter into a contract with another party. To offer (or to make an offer) means to ask a party if they agree to exchange a good or service for something, usually money. If this offer is accepted by the other party then a basic contract is formed, depending on other legal factors being satisfied.
Associated Words: Offered (past simple), Offered (3rd form), Offer (noun), To Accept (verb), Party (noun).

Power of Attorney (noun): This means a document (or a person) which states that a person is legally entitled to enter into contracts or agreements on behalf of someone else. It is common for powers of attorney to be granted when one person is not physically or mentally able to enter into contracts themselves. In the UK is it common for solicitors to act as power of attorney on behalf of their clients.
Associated Words: To be Entitled To (collocation), To Enter Into (collocation).

Pre-Contractual (adjective): All discussions and negotiations that are made before contracts or agreements are signed are called pre-contractual. For instance, pre-contractual negotiations can continue for months before a contract is actually executed.
Associated Words: Pre-contract (noun), To Execute (verb), To Negotiate (verb).

Privity of Contract (collocation): This means that only a party to a contract may benefit from the rights in that contract and have duties and obligations imposed upon them. It means that the parties have privity of contract. There are also some situations in commercial contracts where third parties are also able to benefit from rights in a contract that they are not actually a party to.
Associated Words: Duties and Obligations (noun), Party (noun), Rights (noun), Third Party (noun).

Remedy (noun): This word is used to describe the way a court will try to compensate or resolve the harm or loss that the claimant has suffered. There are three main types of remedy common in commercial contract disputes. The most common remedy is damages. This is monetary compensation awarded to the claimant to compensate them for their loss. The second main type are called equitable remedies, such as an injunction or specific performance. These are court orders that specify that a particular action must be taken or is prohibited. The third main type are declaratory judgments which state the rights or legal relationships between parties.

Associated Words: To Remedy (verb), Damages (noun), Injunction (noun), Specific Performance (noun).

To Renew (verb): In legal English to renew is commonly used when a commercial contract is extended by all the parties on the same (or similar) terms as the original contract.

Associated Words: Renewed (past simple), Renewed (3rd form), Renewal (noun), Party (noun).

To Rent (verb): This means one party pays money to another to use a good or service for a period of time. Most commonly the verb rent is used in relation to property. For instance, "the company rents office premises from the local authority".

Associated Words: Rented (past simple), Rented (3rd form), Rent (noun), Goods (noun), Party (noun).

To Rescind (verb): This verb is used as a remedy to cancel a contract between parties. The principle of the remedy is to put all the parties back in the position they were in before they entered into the contract. Courts may have the power to rescind a contract in certain situations.

Associated Words: Rescinded (past simple), Rescinded (3rd form), Rescission (noun), Remedy (noun).

Restitution (noun): This is a type of remedy from the court commonly used with commercial contracts. Usually the court will order compensation to be paid by the defendant for the loss suffered by the claimant in the form of damages. However, in some situations the loss suffered by the claimant may be very small. The court has the option to order restitution. The law of restitution means that the court orders the defendant to pay any profits that resulted from their breach of contract to the claimant. For example, Mr Burgess issues proceedings against Mr Shaw for breach of contract. Mr Burgess did not actually suffer any loss as a result of Mr Shaw's breach, but if Mr Shaw profited greatly from the result of his breach, then the court can order restitution and order that Mr Shaw pay his profits from his breach of contract to Mr Burgess.

Associated Words: Breach of Contract (collocation), Damages (noun), Remedy (noun).

Specific Performance (noun): This is a remedy from the court that orders a party to do a certain act. Usually specific performance is ordered to make a party fulfil their obligations under a contract. It is an alternative remedy when damages are perhaps not relevant to the claim as the claimant has not actually suffered any loss.

Associated Words: Damages (noun), Fulfil an Obligation (collocation), Remedy (noun).

To Take Instructions (collocation): This collocation is used between a lawyer and their client. It means that the client will tell the lawyer what they wish to do in relation to the legal matter. The lawyer will then be in a position to advise the client.

Uncertainty (noun): In commercial contracts, it is fundamental that the terms, conditions and meanings in the clauses are certain. A contract can be void because of uncertainty. This means that the contract may not be valid because the intentions of the parties or the meanings of the words cannot be interpreted with certainty.

Associated Words: Certainty (noun), To Interpret (verb), Terms and Conditions (collocation), Valid (adjective), Void (adjective).

Unfair Contract Terms (collocation): This collocation is very important in commercial contracts. It is a fundamental principle of consumer contract law that the contract must not be unfair on the consumer. This means that the terms and conditions in the contract must be reasonable and fair for all parties. There is significant statute and common law on what is fair and unfair in commercial contracts.

Associated Words: Consumer Contract (noun), Terms and Conditions (noun).

Unsolicited Goods (noun): These are goods or products that are delivered to someone who has not ordered them. In commercial contracts there may be terms that deal with the situation when goods have been delivered to parties who did not place an order for them. The parties can agree terms to decide in advance what should happen in this situation.
Associated Words: To Deliver (verb), Goods (noun), Party (noun), To Place an Order (collocation).

Valid (Adjective): In commercial contracts valid means that a contract is legally enforceable.
Associated Words: Validity (noun), Invalid (adjective), To Enforce (verb).

3. INTRODUCTORY CONTRACT TERMS

To Accrue (verb): This means to increase. It is usually used in relation to interest on debts or money in arrears. For example, BigCo Inc. borrows £40,000 from Best Bank at an interest rate of 3%. The contract states that BigCo Inc. must pay instalments of £3,000 a month. BigCo Inc. is having financial problems and cannot pay £3,000 every month and so are now in arrears. The contract states that interest will accrue on the amount of money in arrears at a rate of 5%. The amount of money that is in arrears is accruing interest at a higher rate because BigCo Inc. are late with their instalment payments to Small Bank.
Associated Words: To Borrow (verb), Debt (noun), In Arrears (collocation), Interest (noun), Instalments (noun).

To Apply to (phrasal verb): This phrasal verb means that something relates or links to something else. For example, a commercial contract may state, *"This contract applies to the provision of services in Germany only"*. This means that the contract only relates to the provision of services in Germany.
Associated Words: Provision (noun), Service (noun).

Business Day (noun): This means any day that is not a weekend or national holiday. For instance, Christmas Day and New Year's Day are not business days.

By/In Instalments (collocation): This phrase is used in commercial contracts in relation to payment. Payments made in/by instalments are payments that are not made in full but made on a regular basis in a smaller amount. It is common for goods to be paid for in/by instalments and these payments are usually detailed in a schedule at the back of the main contract.
Associated Word: Schedule (noun).

To Collect From (phrasal verb): This means to get something from someone else. For instance, a commercial contract may have a condition that the buyer must collect the goods from the seller at an agreed address.
Associated Word: Condition (noun).

Creditor (person or organisation): A creditor is a person or organisation that is owed money. For example, Mr Smalley borrows £5,000 from Big Bank. Big Bank is the creditor in this transaction because Mr Smalley owes them £5,000. Mr Smalley is called the debtor. In commercial contracts, the creditor may have certain rights connected with the money that they are owed by the debtor, especially if there is a charge on the debt.
Associated Words: Credit (noun), To Borrow (verb), Charge (noun), Debt (noun), Debtor (person or organisation), To Owe (verb).

To be Deemed (collocation): This phrase means to be seen or assumed. For example, if a contract states that the goods are to be deemed as received by the buyer by 27th June, then it means that the goods are seen or assumed as received by the buyer by 27th June. A commercial contract clause may state, "The seller is deemed to have full legal title to the goods". This means that it is assumed that the seller is the full legal owner.
Associated Words: Clause (noun), Goods (noun), Title (noun).

Definitions (noun): This is a section of a commercial contract where the most important terms and phrases are explained in detail. The reason for a definitions section is to avoid misinterpretation or misunderstanding of the fundamental terms of the contract.
Associated Word: Terms (noun).

To Delay (verb): This verb means an event or situation happens later than previously planned.

Duties and Obligations (collocation): This term is one of the most common in commercial contracts. Duties and obligations are the tasks that must be done under the contract. The term means that each duty and obligation is extremely important for the contract to be fulfiled. For example, under a commercial contract for services, it will be a common duty and obligation that the service provided is of a reasonable quality for the purposes required. Other duties and obligations will include payment, delivery of goods, time periods, quality of goods and services, etc. In legal English it is common to hear the phrase "to fulfil duties and obligations". This means to complete or finish them.

Associated Words: Delivery (noun), To Fulfil (verb), Goods (noun), Quality (noun), Services (noun).

Express Terms (noun): An express term is a clause or provision written in the contract. It is clearly stated in the contract and will usually include a duty or obligation to be fulfiled. These terms are specifically negotiated by the parties.
Associated Words: Clause (noun), Duties and Obligations (collocation), Implied Terms (noun).

To Execute (verb): This means to sign and date the contract to confirm all the parties agree to the terms and give the agreement a date.
Associated Words: Executed (past simple), Executed (3rd form), Party (noun).

Forthwith (noun): This means immediately, as soon as reasonably possible or without delay. Legal English has recently tried to move away from the old traditional "legalese" words, such as forthwith, and so any of the above alternatives are acceptable in drafting modern commercial contracts.
Associated Words: To Draft (verb), Legalese (noun).

From Time to Time (collocation): This phrase is commonly used in commercial contracts and means at any time.

Hereunder (noun): This is an old fashioned legalese word meaning somewhere below in this document.

Implied Terms (noun): These terms are not stated or written in the contract, but they still form part of the contractual duties and obligations. For example in sale of goods contracts there is an implied term that the goods must be of reasonable quality and fit for purpose.
Associated Words: Duties and Obligations (collocation), Goods (noun), Quality (noun).

In Arrears (collocation): In arrears means that you owe money that you should have paid before. This phrase is used to describe the situation when a buyer is late with their payments to the seller. For example, company X buys a boat from company Z and must pay company Z $1,200 per month in instalments for 5 years. If company X fails to pay any of the instalments, then it is in arrears. Another common example is when a person or company takes a loan out with a bank. If a person or company misses an instalment or a payment that they should have made, then their account will be in arrears. It is common for commercial contracts to contain a clause that the interest rate will increase on the amount of money that is in arrears.

Associated Words: Clause (noun), Interest (noun), Instalments (noun), Loan (noun), To Owe (verb).

In Respect of (collocation): This is a common phrase in commercial contracts which means connected with or to do with. For example, a clause in a commercial contract may state: *"Party B is to pay all outstanding invoices in respect of the delivered goods within 30 days* of *the date of delivery"*. This means that Party B must pay all outstanding invoices that are connected with the delivered goods within 30 days.

Associated Words: Clause (noun), To Deliver (verb), Goods (noun), Invoice (noun), Outstanding (noun).

Joint and Several Liability (collocation): This phrase means that if there is a group of two or more people who are liable for a debt, then all of the members of the group are liable individually and also together as a group. For example, if Mr and Mrs Benson are liable for damages under a commercial contract, the court may order that the liability is joint and several. This means that Mr Smith is liable for all of the debt, Mrs Smith is liable for all the debt, and together Mr and Mrs Smith are liable for the debt. The court can enforce the judgment against both Mr and Mrs Benson individually or together.

Associated Words: Damages (noun), To Enforce (verb).

To be Made on (phrasal verb): This phrasal verb is used in relation to the date of the contract. It is common to see the phrase *"This agreement is made on 17th February 2014"*. This means that the agreement was executed on this date.

Associated Words: Was Made On (past simple), To Execute (verb).

Neither Party (collocation): This term is used to suggest that if there are two parties to the agreement, then both parties do not have to do something. For example, a common clause may state, "*Neither party is responsible for insuring the property*". This means that both parties are not responsible for insuring the property.
Associated Words: Clause (noun), Insurance (noun).

Notwithstanding/Notwithstanding the Foregoing (noun): This is an old legalese word meaning despite or in spite of. The use of this term can complicate clauses and should be avoided from a drafting point of view. For example, older commercial contracts may include this term in some clauses, for instance "SmallCo is not permitted to consume alcohol on the premises. Notwithstanding the foregoing, SmallCo may hold private social events on the premises for up to a maximum of 20 people". The clause means that despite not being allowed alcohol on the property, the company may use the property for private social events for a small number of people.
Associated Words: Clause (noun). To Draft (verb), Premises (noun).

Outstanding (adjective): The word outstanding describes a situation when something is owed. It is usually used to describe a debt owed. In commercial contracts the word is commonly used in relation to money owed by one party to another. If the buyer owes the seller money, for instance for an unpaid invoice, then the buyer has an outstanding debt to the seller.
Associated Words: Debt (noun), Invoice (noun), To Owe (verb), Party (noun).

Penalty Clause (noun): A penalty clause states that in the event of a particular situation, an amount of money is to be paid as a penalty (for instance, breach of restrictive covenant). However, it is important to note that penalty clauses in commercial contracts can be unenforceable. The reason for this is that any attempt to estimate loss of a breach of a term or condition of the contract must be in relation to compensating the injured party, rather than punishing the party in breach. It is important to remember that when drafting commercial contracts (or negotiating them) that penalties for breaches of contracts may not be enforceable.
Associated Words: To Breach (verb), To Draft (verb), To Enforce (verb),

Injured Party (noun), To Negotiate (verb).

Price (noun): This means the cost or the value of the goods or service provided in the contract. It is naturally, one of the most important terms and negotiating aspects of all commercial contracts.
Associated Words: Goods (noun), To Negotiate (verb), Service (noun), Terms (noun).

To Rely On/Upon (phrasal verb): In commercial contracts it is common for clauses to be "relied on or upon". For instance, a party will rely on representations made by another party to enter into the contract. In this commercial contracts context, the phrasal verb to rely on means to trust and depend on a representation or clause in an agreement.
Associated Words: Relied On/Upon (past simple), Relied On/Upon (3rd form), Clause (noun), Party (noun), Representation (noun).

Representations (noun): In legal English a representation is a factual statement made by a party that informs and persuades another party to enter into the contract. It is common for legal proceedings to arise because of representations (or "misrepresentations"). A misrepresentation is a factual statement that is later found to be false or a lie. In legal English is it common for a claim in tort for misrepresentation to be brought. For example, ABC Inc. and XYZ plc are negotiating over a contract for the supply of cars. ABC Inc. manufactures the cars and XYZ plc want to buy them from ABC and then sell them to customers. ABC make a representation to XYZ that all the cars were manufactured after 2010. There is no term in the contract about the age of the cars. XYZ buy the cars from ABC and later discover that they were all made in 2007. XYZ can bring a claim against ABC in tort for misrepresentation.
Associated Words: To Claim (verb), To Negotiate (verb), Tort (noun).

To Set Out (phrasal verb): This phrasal verb is very common in a commercial contract and means that something is stated or written somewhere else in the contract. For instance, a common clause is "The parties agree to fulfil all their duties and obligations as set out in this agreement". This means that the parties agree to complete their duties, which

have been stated or written in full somewhere else in the contract.
Associated Words: Duties and Obligations (collocation), To Fulfil (verb).

Schedule (noun): This is a part of a contract usually found at the end or added as an appendix. Schedules are used to set out information that does not naturally fit into the main contract or agreement. For example, dates, prices, lists of products and other details are commonly added to contracts in the form of schedules.

Subject to (collocation): This collocation means that something will happen if something else happens also. For example, a clause in a contract may state *"the buyer agrees to purchase the goods subject to them being of a reasonable quality for their purpose"*. Here the collocation 'subject to' means that the purchase of the goods depends on them being of a reasonable quality for the purposes of their use.
Associated Words: Clause (noun), Goods (noun), To Purchase (verb), Quality (noun).

Sums Due (collocation): This means amount owed. For instance a commercial contract will usually state an exact date when payment must be made. Another way of saying this is that the sums are due on this date.
Associated Word: To Owe (verb).

To Supply (verb): This means to give or provide. It is one of the fundamental verbs used in commercial contracts for goods and services.
Associated Words: Supplied (past simple), Supplied (3rd form), Supply (noun), Supplier (person/organisation).

Term of Art (collocation): These are industry specific terms. Legal English has many terms of art which are specific to this industry and there will be many that are specific to commercial contracts. Examples of terms of art in commercial contracts are force majeure, boilerplate clause, warranties and guarantees.
Associated Words: Boilerplate Clause (noun), Force Majeure (noun), Guarantee (noun), Warranty (noun).

Thereof (noun): This is an old legalese word and means about something recently mentioned or said. For example, an old-fashioned legalese clause may state, *"The boxes will be delivered in excellent condition together with the contents thereof"*. The word thereof is talking about the contents of the boxes mentioned at the beginning of the clause.

Associated Words: Clause (noun), To Deliver (verb), Legalese (noun).

Time is of the Essence (collocation): This is a very common phrase in commercial contracts. It means that time is at the very centre of the contract and should be treated as one of the most important concepts. This has implications on the importance of delivery time, payment periods, etc. The phrase suggests that there will be serious consequences for breaches of terms and conditions that involve time.

Associated Words: To Breach (verb), Terms and Conditions (noun).

Under/At Clause (collocation): This means that a specific clause is referred to. For example, a client may ask their lawyer *"I don't understand the provisions under clause 5.3 in the contract"* or a lawyer may state *"Your client is in material breach of contract as they failed to pay the sums due under clause 3.4 of the contract"*. The phrase "under clause 3.4" means that this specific clause is being looked at or referred to.

Associated Words: Breach of Contract (noun), Clause (noun).

4 DUTIES AND OBLIGATIONS

All Reasonable Endeavours (collocation): Parties to a commercial contract should enter into the contract in good faith. This phrase states that a party (or parties) will do their best where reasonably possible. The phrase is used to make sure that a party fulfils a duty or obligation, or at least to use a reasonable amount of effort to fulfil them. This phrase is sometimes subject to negotiation as 'reasonable' is not a strong word in this situation. For instance, if you are asking another party to do something under the contract, then you would argue for the phrase 'all endeavours' or 'all best endeavours'. This is much stronger. However, if you are the party who must do something under the contract then you would argue that you should use 'all reasonable endeavours' as this obligation is easier to fulfil.

Associated Words: All Endeavours (collocation), All Best Endeavours (collocation), Duties and Obligations (collocation), Enter into a Contract (collocation), To Fulfil (verb), Good Faith (noun), Negotiation (noun), Party (noun).

Bill of Lading (noun): This is a type of contract used in shipping contracts. The contract is usually in the form of a receipt that the carrier of the goods (the ship) will give to the seller (or the agent of the seller) as evidence that the goods have been loaded and are being transported to the buyer. It is a legally binding document and can confirm the fulfilment of a contractual obligation. It can also be attached to the primary contract. The bill of lading can also confirm legal title of the goods, used as evidence for tax and insurance purposes and even include terms and conditions regarding quality and fitness for purpose. The receipt is also sent to the buyer in order to guarantee payment when the goods are delivered.

Associated Words: To Bind (verb), To Deliver (verb), Fit for Purpose (collocation), To Fulfil (verb), Goods (noun), Guarantee (noun), Insurance (noun), Obligations (noun), Quality (noun), Terms and Conditions (noun), Title (noun).

Carriage by Sea (collocation): This is a legal English phrase commonly found in commercial contract that means that the goods subject to the contract are being transported by ship. This can have consequences in relation to insurance of the goods while they are being transported and this issue will also have to be dealt with in the contract.

Associated Words: Goods (noun), Insurance (noun).

Charter Party (noun): This is a type of commercial contract entered into between a ship-owner and a charterer. Under this contract, a ship is let or hired for the carriage of goods by sea on an agreed journey for a specific period of time.

Associated Words: Charterer (noun), Carriage by sea, Goods (noun), To Hire (verb), To Let (verb).

To Clear Funds (collocation): This means that payment for the goods or services has arrived in the bank account of the seller. Once the payment appears in the seller's bank account, the money has 'cleared'.

Associated Word: Goods (noun).

Commission (noun): This means that a person is paid a part or all of their salary as a percentage of the amount of goods that they sell. For instance, Mr Grant sells cars. He receives a basic salary plus 20% of the value of every car that he sells. This 20% is called commission.

Contingent Obligations (noun): This means that a duty or obligation is dependent on another event or situation happening first. For example, a contingent obligation may be if a buyer wishes to purchase more goods, then they can do so at the same price, if the buyer gives the seller two weeks notice. This is a typical example of a contingent obligation.

Associated Words: Goods (noun), Notice (noun), To Purchase (verb).

Data Protection (noun): This means that when a consumer purchases a good or service, the personal data and information given to the seller must be protected and kept confidential unless the buyer gives the seller permission to use the information given. This is common with distance selling and e-commerce commercial contracts as the buyer will usually give their email address and bank details to the seller over the internet. There may be clauses in commercial contracts that provide for the seller protecting the buyer's personal data.

Associated Words: Clause (noun), Distance selling (noun), E-commerce (noun), Goods (noun), To Purchase (verb).

To Default/To be In Default (collocation): This means that you failed to do something under the contract. For example, if the buyer does not pay an invoice on time then they are in default of the payment.
Associated Word: Invoice (noun).

Default Provisions (noun): Default provisions in commercial contracts are the situations that exist or will happen if the parties do not vary, change or alter them.
Associated Words: Provisions (noun), To Vary (verb).

Defective Product (noun): This means that products or goods are not of reasonable quality or not fit for their purpose. Commercial contracts usually contain a clause dealing with what the parties should do if a product is defective.
Associated Words: Clause (noun), Fit for Purpose (collocation), Goods (noun), Quality (noun).

Description (noun): In a commercial contract the good or service must be accurately described. This means that the seller must truthfully explain to the buyer what the product is or what the service will provide. The description of the good or service for sale is very important in commercial contracts because the buyer will rely on this when making a decision to enter into the contract. It is important that the seller is honest with the description because claims for misrepresentation can be brought if the buyer feels that the good or service was not as described in the contract.
Associated Words: To Describe (verb), To Enter Into (phrasal verb), Goods (noun), Misrepresentation (noun).

To Discharge (verb): This verb means to end the contract and for the parties to be free of their contractual obligations.
Associated Words: Obligation (noun), Party (noun).

Encumbrance (noun): This means a burden or restriction. It is commonly used in relation to property. For instance, if Company A wishes to buy a property to use as their offices, then need to check that the land is free from all encumbrances. Encumbrances can include third party rights or charges that another party may have over the property.

Fair Wear and Tear (collocation): This phrase means that a product will usually become dirty, marked, scratched or damaged during its natural life. In commercial contracts there is usually a provision that states that fair wear and tear is normal and that it is a consequence of normal use. The phrase is used so that a buyer cannot bring a claim against the seller because the product becomes dirty or marked through normal everyday use.
Associated Word: Provision (noun).

Fit for Purpose (collocation): This means that the good or service for sale is suitable for the intended use of the good or service. This is connected to the concept that the good or service must be of a reasonable quality and this is usually an implied term of a commercial contract.
Associated Words: Goods (noun), Implied Term (noun).

To be Free from (phrasal verb): Commercial contracts usually contain a number of warranties, indemnities and guarantees. These can be in relation to one party confirming that the goods are in good condition and they are fit for purpose. Commercial contracts will usually use the phrase "to be free from" to draft a warranty or guarantee. For example, the buyer of goods will usually ask the seller to confirm that the goods "*are free from all encumbrances, defects and third party rights*". This means that the goods are clean and without any problems or ownership issues. It is common for such language to be used when drafting warranties, indemnities and guarantees in commercial contracts.
Associated Words: Defective (adjective), Encumbrance (noun), Fit for purpose (collocation), Goods (noun), Guarantee (noun), Indemnity (noun), Warranty (noun).

Indemnity (noun): This is a term in a commercial contract that states that a party will pay an amount of money if a certain condition in the contract is not completed or later found to be not true. For example, if Company ABC want to buy Company DEF then Company ABC will ask Company DEF to grant them an indemnity for any tax liabilities that Company DEF owe to the tax authorities. This means that if Company DEF have any unpaid tax liabilities then Company DEF must indemnify Company ABC for the total amount of these tax liabilities.

Associated Words: Condition (noun), Party (noun).

Innominate Term (noun): This is a term in a commercial contract that is not a condition or a warranty.

Associated Words: Condition (noun), Warranty (noun).

In Relation to (collocation): This means that something is connected or linked to something else. For instance, it is common to see phrases such as *"The Buyer is relying on the warranty provided at clause 6.3 in relation to the condition of the goods"*. This means that the warranty at clause 6.3 is connected or discusses the condition of the goods. It is a very helpful phrase to connect one issue to another.

Associated Words: Clause (noun), Goods (noun), Warranty (noun).

Invoice (noun): This is a document used to detail the products, goods or services that have been ordered by the buyer. Usually, payment details are also set out in an invoice.

Associated Word: Goods (noun).

Joint Obligations (noun): This means that two or more parties share a duty or obligation under the contract.

Associated Words: Duties and Obligations (collocation), Party (noun), Under the Contract (collocation).

Obligations Under (e.g. clause 5.2) (collocation): This phrase means to refer to a particular clause or term in the contract. Lawyers in correspondence often use this term. For example, *"We refer to your client's failure to fulfil their contractual obligations under clause 7.3 of the Agreement"*. The phrase "under clause [___]" is a useful way to refer to a clause in a contract.

Associated Words: Clause (noun), To Fulfil (verb), Obligation (noun).

To Pass (verb): In legal English this has a similar meaning to transfer. For instance, the phrase "to pass legal title" means to transfer legal title. "To pass risk" is also a common legal English phrase used in commercial contracts and means that risk is transferred from one party to another.

Associated Words: Passed (past simple), Passed (3rd form), Title (noun), Risk (noun).

Premises (noun): This is a formal and legal English word that means property or building.

Quality (noun): This means the standard of the good or service. It is usually an implied term in a commercial contract that the good or service is of a reasonable quality for the intended use.

Associated Words: Goods (noun), Implied Term (noun).

Restrictive Covenants (noun): This means that a party is forbidden or not allowed to do something stated in the contract. Restrictive covenants are usually included in employment and commercial property contracts. For example, in employment contracts there are usually confidentiality clauses that state that after an employee leaves their job, they must not release any trade secrets or confidential information about the employer. This is a type of restrictive covenant.

Associated Words: Confidentiality (noun), Party (noun).

Right of Cancellation (collocation): Some commercial contracts include a clause that allows the parties a chance to cancel the contract in certain situations. This is known as the right of cancellation.

Associated Words: Clause (noun), Party (noun).

Risk (noun): This means a chance of danger or loss. Risk is a very important concept in commercial contracts and during negotiations. Both buyers and sellers must be aware of the potential risks of entering into the contract. Due to the nature of risk in commercial contracts, parties will include warranties, indemnities, guarantees and covenants to reduce their risk.

Associated Words: To Risk (verb), Covenant (noun), To Enter Into (phrasal verb), Guarantee (noun), Indemnity (noun), To Negotiate (verb), Warranty

(noun).

Sample (noun): This is a small part, piece or an example of the goods or products for sale under a commercial contract. For example, when a shop wishes to buy an amount of fruit from a wholesaler, it is common for the shop to ask for samples of the fruit to be sent and tested before entering into a contract.
Associated Word: Goods (noun).

To be of Satisfactory Quality (collocation): This is a standard phrase in commercial contracts that means that the goods or services being provided under the contract must be of a reasonable quality and fit for the purpose of the contract.
Associated Words: Fit for Purpose (collocation), Goods (noun), Quality (noun).

Termination (noun): This means to end or finish. In legal English the word termination is used when a commercial contract comes to an end. There are many different ways of terminating a contract and each one will carry its own legal consequences. Examples of contract termination include material breach of contract, fixed-term expiration and force majeure.
Associated Words: To Terminate (verb), Terminated (past simple), Terminated (3rd form), Breach of Contract (collocation), Expiration (noun), Fixed-Term (noun), Force Majeure (noun), Material Breach (collocation).

Terms and Conditions (noun): These are the requirements and tasks to be completed under the contract. The terms and conditions section of the contract will usually be the longest part. This is where the duties and obligations of the parties are explained. It will also set out the possible consequences for not fulfiling the duties and obligations, for instance it will detail the warranties, indemnities and guarantees of the contract.
Associated Words: Clause (noun), Guarantee (noun), Indemnity (noun), Set Out (phrasal verb), Under the Contract (collocation), Warranty (noun).

Value Added Tax "VAT" (noun): This is a tax placed on goods or services which are paid for by the buyer. VAT is like a sales tax in that ultimately only the end consumer is taxed. There are strict rules and regulations in most jurisdictions that state which goods and services are allowed to charge VAT and which are not.

Associated Words: Goods (noun), Jurisdiction (noun).

Variation (noun): This word means a change or alteration. Many commercial contracts need to be changed or altered at some point and so most agreements will include a variation clause. This allows the parties to agree the terms of variation in writing and for that change to be fully implemented into the main contract.

Associated Words: To Vary (verb), Varied (past simple), Varied (3rd form), Clause (noun), Party (noun).

Warranty (noun): This is a promise or guarantee made by a party that a fact (or facts) in a contract are true. Warranties are usually given from the seller to the buyer in relation to the quality of goods and services and legal title of goods for sale. For example, Mr Bennett wishes to buy a car from Mrs Gordon. Mr Bennett wants to be sure that the car is less than 5 years old and in reasonable condition for use. Mr Bennett will ask Mrs Gordon to include an express warranty in the contract that the car is less than 5 years old and in reasonable condition for use. Mr Bennett then decides to buy the car. If the car is not less than 5 years old or not in reasonable condition for use, Mr Bennett will be able to use this warranty if he wishes to bring a civil claim against Mrs Gordon. There are two main types of warranty. An express warranty is a warranty stated in the contract. An implied warranty is a warranty that is not stated in the contract, but can be relied on if it is reasonable to do so. For example, a common implied warranty is that the goods on sale are the same as the goods that are advertised.

Associated Words: Goods (noun), Guarantee (noun), Title (noun), Party (noun), Quality (noun).

5 BOILERPLATE CLAUSES

Applicable Law/Governing Law (noun): This means the law of the country that will govern the contract. The two phrases are very similar in meaning and only differ when used in different contexts. In a commercial contract, the phrase governing law will usually be used. The parties use this clause to state which country's laws (e.g. the laws of England and Wales) will govern the contract. Sometimes, in the event of a dispute, the phrase applicable law is used. It is important to distinguish between applicable law/governing law and jurisdiction.
Associated Words: Clause (noun), Dispute (noun), Party (noun).

Assignment (noun): This clause deals with the parties transferring the rights (and liabilities) under the contract to another party. Another term for this is Novation.
Associated Words: To Assign (verb), Clause (noun), Novation (noun).

Boilerplate Clause (noun): This is a standard clause in a commercial contract which is commonly found in most agreements. Examples of boilerplate clauses are confidentiality, force majeure, governing law and jurisdiction.
Associated Words: Clause (noun), Confidentiality (noun), Force Majeure (noun), Governing Law (noun), Jurisdiction (noun).

Confidentiality (noun): This commercial contract clause will state that the contents and information that appears in the contract and any supplementary documents to it will remain secret and confidential between the parties. Confidentiality clauses are very common in employment contracts and usually allow for a period of time after the employee leaves the position for all confidential and secret information to not be disclosed.
Associated Word: Clause (noun).

Conflict of Laws (noun): This clause deals with the situation where there is a dispute over which laws govern the contract. Commercial contracts may contain a clause that expressly states which country's law will govern the contract and this clause is called an applicable law clause or governing law clause.

Associated Words: Applicable Law (noun), Clause (noun), Dispute (noun), Governing Law (noun).

Entire Agreement (noun): This clause states that only the clauses written in the contract are valid. All pre-contractual discussions, negotiations and representations are excluded from the contract. It is common for this clause to try to prevent any reliance on misrepresentations made before the execution of the commercial contract.

Associated Words: Clause (noun), To Execute (verb), Misrepresentation (noun), To Negotiate (verb), Valid (adjective).

Exclusion (noun): This clause attempts to restrict the rights of parties' liabilities under the contract. It is common for parties to try to prevent other parties enforcing their rights under the contract by including an exclusion of liability clause. There are statutory limitations on what types of liability can be excluded in commercial contracts.

Associated Words: Clause (noun), To Enforce (verb), Liability (noun), Rights (noun).

Exclusivity (noun): This means that one party to a commercial contract will have the exclusive right to do something (usually sell goods) in a certain geographical area or jurisdiction. Exclusivity clauses are very common in commercial contracts for goods because it provides the seller with certainty that the buyer will only sell goods provided by the seller in a specific place. The clause can also be an advantage for the buyer as the contract could include an exclusivity clause that the seller will only sell to the buyer (and no-one else) in this specific jurisdiction.

Associated Words: Goods (noun), Jurisdiction (noun).

Force Majeure (noun): This is a very common clause in commercial contracts because it states that the parties become free from their contractual duties and obligations if specific or extraordinary situations make it impossible for the parties to fulfil their obligations. Common examples that are included in a force majeure clause are wars, riots, strikes and natural disasters (also known as Acts of God).

Associated Words: Clause (noun), Duties and Obligations (collocation), To Fulfil (verb).

To Give Warranties/Indemnities/Guarantees (collocation): This collocation is used when one party provides or grants a warranty, indemnity or guarantee to another party. It is commonly used in pre-contractual negotiations and in written commercial contracts. It is the correct form to use when referring to these representations and statements in commercial contracts. For example, "Company A gave a warranty to Company B that they possessed legal title to the goods".

Associated Words: Goods (noun), Guarantee (noun), Indemnity (noun), To Negotiate (verb), Pre-Contractual (noun), Representation (noun), Title (noun), Warranty (noun).

Good Faith (noun): To act in good faith means to behave in an honest way without intending to cause any unfair influence or disadvantage onto another party. It is common in many jurisdictions that an implied term of a commercial contract is to act in good faith.

Associated Words: To Act in Good Faith (collocation), Jurisdiction (noun), Party (noun).

INCO terms (noun): Inco terms (or International Commercial Terms) are internationally recognized rules for conducting business using common commercial terms and procedures. Commercial contracts that cover different jurisdictions, especially, shipping contracts, commonly use INCO terms as their main standard terms and conditions of trade.

Associated Words: Jurisdiction (noun), Terms and Conditions (noun).

Limitation (noun): Parties can include a provision that limits the amount of damages that can be claimed in the event of a breach contract. Alternatively, parties can also include a time limitation in the contract to state a time limit for any claims to be issued in relation to the contract.

Associated Words: Breach of Contract (collocation), Provision (noun).

Notice (noun): This means stating or notifying that something has been done or a party wishes to do something. Notice provisions in a contract usually relate to specific parts of information that must be given to another party. For example, some commercial contracts can be terminated upon notice. This means that one party states to the other that they wish to end the contract. There will usually be a notice period for this event for example; a contract may state that the notice period for terminating the contract is four weeks. This is called giving notice.
Associated Words: To Give Notice (collocation), Notice Period (noun), Provision (noun), To Terminate (verb).

Restraint of Trade (noun): This clause deals with the situation when one party tries to limit the business, trade or activity of another. Commercial contracts must be careful if a party wishes to include a restraint of trade clause, as it must not conflict with anti-competition law. However, this type of clause is commonly found in employment contracts.
Associated Word: Clause (noun).

Set-off (noun): This is a provision a commercial contract where the parties agree that if a party defaults under the contract, then any money owed to the defaulting party does not have to be paid.
Associated Words: To Default (verb), To Owe (verb).

Severability (noun): This means that if a clause or section of the contract is found to be illegal or unenforceable then the other parts of the contract are still valid and will still apply. It is common for contracts to include a severability clause because usually contracts can continue to operate without the illegal clause.
Associated Words: Clause (noun), To Enforce (verb).

Void (adjective): This means that a clause, term or provision in the contract is unenforceable and has no legal effect.
Associated Words: Clause (noun), To Enforce (verb), Provision (noun), Term (noun).

6. GLOSSARY

Types of Contracts

Agency Agreement
Consumer Credit Agreement
Distance Selling
Distribution Agreement
E-commerce
Franchise
To Hire
Hire Agreement
Hire-Purchase Agreements
Insurance
Lease
To License
Loan Agreement
Marketing
Outsourcing
Sale of Goods
Subrogation
Supply of Services

How is a Contract Created?

To Accept
To Affirm
To Amend
Authority to Contract
To Breach
Capacity to Contract
To Consent
Consideration
Damages
To Dispute
Duress

To Enforce
To Enter Into
To Expire
Frustration
Heads of Terms
Injunction
Intention
To Let
Liquidated Damages
Mitigation of Loss
To Negotiate
To Offer
Power of Attorney
Pre-Contractual
Privity of Contract
Remedy
To Renew
To Rent
To Rescind
Restitution
Specific Performance
To Take Instructions
Uncertainty
Unfair Contract Terms
Unsolicited Goods
Valid

Introductory Contract Terms

To Accrue
To Apply to
Business Day
By/In Instalments
To Collect From
Creditor
To be Deemed

Definitions
To Delay
Duties and Obligations
Express Terms
To Execute
Forthwith
From Time to Time
Hereunder
Implied Terms.
In Arrears
In Respect of
Joint and Several Liability
To be Made on
Neither Party
Notwithstanding/Notwithstanding the Foregoing
Outstanding
Penalty Clause
Price
To Rely On/Upon
Representations
To Set Out
Schedule
Subject to
Sums Due
To Supply
Term of Art
Thereof
Time is of the Essence
Under/At Clause

Duties and Obligations

All Reasonable Endeavours
Bill of Lading
Carriage by Sea
Charter Party

To Clear Funds
Commission
Contingent Obligations
Data Protection
To Default/To be In Default
Default Provisions
Defective Product
Description
To Discharge
Encumbrance
Fair Wear and Tear
Fit for Purpose
To be Free from
Guarantee
Indemnity
Innominate Term
In Relation to
Invoice
Joint Obligations
Liable
Obligations Under
To Pass
Premises
Quality
Restrictive Covenants
Right of Cancellation
Risk
Sample
To be of Satisfactory Quality
Termination
Terms and Conditions
Title to Goods
Trade Description
Value Added Tax "VAT"
Variation
Warranty

Boilerplate Clauses

Applicable Law/Governing Law
Assignment
Boilerplate Clause
Confidentiality
Conflict of Laws
Entire Agreement
Exclusion
Exclusivity
Force Majeure
To Give Warranties/Indemnities/Guarantees
Good Faith
INCO terms
Limitation
Notice
Restraint of Trade
Set-off
Severability
Void

DRAFTING COMMERCIAL CONTRACTS

7. EXERCISES

TRUE OR FALSE

Decide if these sentences are true or false (answers are at the back of the book):

1. A distance-selling contract is a contract that is entered into without the parties meeting each other face to face. Such contracts can be made over the internet or over the phone.

2. A company (A) grants a licence to another company (B) to sell, manufacture and distribute company A's products. Company B will usually use company A's method, trademarks and technology and will be paid a royalty or commission from the profit. This type of commercial contract is called a marketing agreement.

3. An agreement for the use of property or land for a fixed period of time is called a lease.

4. Under an intellectual property licence agreement, the licensor gives permission to the licensee to use its intellectual property for a period of time. Under a standard licence agreement legal title will pass from the licensor to the licensee.

5. Common examples of outsourcing agreements are for IT services, telephone call centres and basic office administration. This means that an external provider is responsible for supplying these services.

6. To alter is the correct verb to use in legal English if a commercial contract needs to be changed.

7. Consideration is required for a commercial contract to be legally binding and enforceable. Consideration means that both parties receive something as a result of the transaction. Without consideration, a commercial contract is void.

8. In legal English, the verb to enforce means that the contract (or a clause in the contract) is legal and binding and can be used or relied on in a court of law.

9. For a liquidated damages clause to be valid in a commercial contract, the amount of the damages must be a genuine pre-estimate of loss.

10. The law of rescission means that the court orders the defendant to pay any profits that resulted from their breach of contract to the claimant.

11. Any day that is not a weekend or national holiday is called a business day.

12. The section of a commercial contract where the most important terms and phrases are explained in detail to avoid misinterpretation or misunderstanding is called the recitals.

13. The verb to execute means to sign and date the contract to confirm all the parties agree to the terms and give the agreement a date.

14. In some commercial contracts a clause may state that where there is a group of two or more people who are liable for payment under a contract, all of the members of the group are liable individually and also together as a group. This is called joint and individual liability.

15. The general legal English term that means the cost or the value of the goods or service provided in the contract is the price.

16. The legal English phrase commonly found in commercial contracts that means that the goods subject to the contract are being transported by ship or boat is shipment by sea.

17. Mrs Black sells mobile phones. She receives a basic salary plus 15% of the value of every mobile phone that she sells. This 15% is called commission.

18. An encumbrance is a third party right or charge that another party may have over property or land.

19. Indemnities, warranties and guarantees are synonyms. Their meanings are the same when used in commercial contracts.

20. To pass risk is a common legal English phrase used in commercial contracts and means that risk is transferred from one party to another.

VOCABULARY GAP FILL

Complete the sentences with the missing word or phrase (answers are at the back of the book):

1. An _____ agreement is an arrangement between two parties where one party (the "principal") asks another party (the "agent") to represent them and create contractual legal relationships with a third party.

2. The general term for trading over the internet is called e-_____.

3. The verb commonly used in legal English which means paying money to borrow something from someone or to use a product or service temporarily is to _____.

4. There are many different types of _____ agreement and each type has very specific conditions that must be met in order for compensation to be paid for any loss suffered. Usually, the customer will pay a premium every month to be covered by a policy.

5. _____ is when a third party is given the rights or remedies of a claimant against a defendant. Under this doctrine a claimant may not claim for the same loss if they have previously transferred this right to a third party (for example, an insurance company).

6. A common remedy that is available to a party is to ask the court to _____ the contract. This means that the court makes a declaration that the contract is valid and enforceable.

7. Common phrases used in commercial contracts are "_____ of terms and conditions" or "_____ of obligations". This word means that something is broken or that a party has not done something that they should have done.

8. _____ means that a contract will be discharged because an event or situation caused the main duties and obligations of the contract to be impossible to be fulfiled.

9. The name of the remedy available from the court that states that a party must do something or stop from doing something is an _____.

10. _____ of contract means that only a party to a contract may benefit from the rights in that contract or have duties and obligations imposed upon them.

11. My contract with the bank states that *"Interest will* _____ *on the amount of money in arrears at a rate of 6%"*. This means that if I am late with my loan payments to the bank, they will charge extra interest on the amount of money that is late.

12. A _____ is a person or organisation who is owed money. In relation to loans, this is usually a bank.

13. If a person or company misses an instalment or a payment that they should have made, then their account will be _____. It is common for commercial contracts to contain a clause the extra interest rate will increase on this amount of money.

14. In legal English, if a contract states that _____ ___ _____ _____ _____ _____ then there is a suggestion that there will be serious consequences for breaches of terms and conditions that involve time.

15. *"The seller must use* _____ _____ _____ *to deliver the goods within 14 days of the date of the order"*. This means that the seller must do everything that is reasonably possible to fulfil this obligation under the contract.

16. If a buyer does not pay an invoice on time then they are _____ _____ _____ the payment.

17. In commercial contracts, products or goods which are not of reasonable quality or not fit for their purpose are called _____ products.

18. To be legally responsible for an act or omission that causes harm or loss to another is to be _____ for that act or omission.

19. In some employment contracts there are confidentiality clauses that state that after an employee leaves their job, they must not release any trade secrets or confidential information about the employer. This type of clause is called a _____ covenant.

20. There are two main types of_____   _____. The "express" type is stated in the contract, while the "implied" type is not stated in the contract but can be relied on if it is reasonable to do so. For example, a common example of the implied type is that the goods on sale are the same as the goods that are advertised.

PREPOSITION GAP FILL

Complete the sentences using the correct preposition (answers are at the back of the book):

1. A party must have authority _____ contract to enter into a legally binding contract. This means that they must have the right to sign the contract, either for themselves or for an organisation.

2. One of the most common types of commercial contracts are for the sale _____ goods or services.

3. The phrase "to enter _____" is used in commercial contracts to describe the act of agreeing to negotiate or agreeing to contract with another party.

4. If a party does not have capacity _____ contract then it is not legally binding on that party. Common examples of parties who do not have capacity to contract are children and people who are mentally impaired.

5. The document that sets out the basic terms of a contract, especially for pre-contractual negotiations is called the heads _____ terms.

6. The concept in common law that means that a person who has suffered loss must take reasonable action to stop or reduce any further loss or damage is called mitigation _____ loss.

7. If a person is not physically or mentally able to enter into a commercial contract themselves, it is possible for them to grant their solicitor or another individual a power _____ attorney. This means that a person is legally entitled to enter into contracts or agreements on behalf of someone else.

8. *"This contract for the sale of goods listed in Appendix A of this agreement applies _____ the provision of services in the European Union only".*

9. It is common for commercial contracts to attach a payment schedule to the back of the main contract if payment for the goods or services are made _____ instalments.

10. *"The buyer must collect the goods _____ the seller at the seller's address stated above* *within 14 days of the date of the invoice".*

11. _____ respect of is a common phrase used in commercial contracts. It is a phrase that means connected to something. For example, a clause may state "The buyer is responsible for payment of all VAT and excise duties __ respect of the purchased goods".

12. A commercial contract will usually start with the date. Common wording for this could be *"This agreement is made _____ 28th July 2014."*

13. Your client is in breach of contract. They failed to pay for the invoices for the goods by the due date. Our client will rely _____ clause 4.7 of the contract where this is clearly stated.

14. The force majeure provisions can be found _____ clause 13 of the contract.

15. Fit _____ purpose means that the goods or services for sale is suitable for the intended use of the goods or services. This is usually an implied term of a commercial contract.

16. My client insists that the goods sold by your client are free ___ all encumbrances, defects and third party rights.

17. If a contact states that *"The guarantee given at clause 5.2 is provided __ relation to the return or refund policy only"* then this means that the guarantee provided at clause 5.2 is connected only to the return or refund policy.

18. To be __ satisfactory quality means that the goods or services being provided under the contract must be of a reasonable quality and fit for the purpose of the contract.

19. Commercial contracts will usually include a clause that states that the seller warrants that they have legal title _____ the goods. This means that they are the legal owner of the goods for sale and that they have the right to sell them.

20. *"All the company's directors have the required authority to execute contracts with the seller from time _____ time."*

COLLOCATION GAP FILL

Complete the sentences using the correct collocation (answers are at the back of the book):

1. A contract where a third party (for example, a financial institution) agrees to finance the purchase of goods or services is called a consumer _____ agreement.

2. Under a _____ agreement, a third party agrees to market and sell goods using their own brand name. The third party is responsible for marketing and delivering the goods to the buyer.

3. A contract between a person who pays to use a product or service for a period of time is called a _____ agreement. These contracts are commonly used for cars and other vehicles.

4. The common contract between a buyer and seller for products or things for sale is called a sale of _____ contract.

5. A standard contract for the _____ of services needs to include terms and conditions for price, inflation, third party costs, transport costs, development and improvement costs, term, termination, quality of the services to be provided, exclusivity and dispute resolution.

6. In legal English, the collocation to _____ instructions means the client will tell their lawyer what they want the lawyer to do and what to include in a contract.

7. Goods or products that are delivered to someone who has not ordered them are called _____ goods.

8. "_____ party may use the premises between the hours of 10pm and 6am on any day". This means that both parties are not allowed to use the property at the stated time.

9. A common commercial contract clause is "*The parties agree to fulfil all their duties and obligations as _____ out in this agreement*". This means that the parties agree to complete their duties, which have been stated or written in full somewhere else in the contract.

10. Industry specific terms are called terms of _____ in legal English. Examples of these in commercial contracts are force majeure, boilerplate clause, warranties and indemnities.

11. A bill of _____ is a document used in shipping contracts. It is usually in the form of a receipt that the carrier of the goods (the ship) will give to the seller (or the agent of the seller) as evidence that the goods have been loaded and are being transported to the buyer. It is a legally binding document and can confirm the fulfilment of a contractual obligation.

12. To _____ funds is the legal English phrase that means payment for the goods or services safely arrives in the bank account of the seller.

13. If a product becomes dirty, marked, scratched or damaged during its natural life, then there may be provisions in the contract that deal with fair wear and _____.

14. Commercial contracts usually include a clause that allows the parties a chance to cancel the contract in certain situations. This is known as the _____ of cancellation.

15. A _____ agreement is a contract where the debtor will borrow money from the creditor and agrees to pay the money back, usually in instalments, plus interest for an agreed period of time.

16. A tax placed on goods or services which are paid for by the final consumer or buyer is known as VAT. Its full name is value _____ tax.

17. The collocation used in legal English when one party provides or grants a warranty, indemnity or guarantee to another party is to _____ a warrant, indemnity or guarantee.

18. If a party tries to limit the business, trade or activity of another, then this clause is called a _____ of trade clause.

19. A set-_____ provision in a commercial contract is where the parties agree that if a party defaults under the contract, then any money owed to the defaulting party does not have to be paid.

20. An agreement where a hirer has the option to buy the goods after a period of time, or after a certain amount of the loan has been re-paid is called a hire-_____ agreement.

REPLACE THE INCORRECT WORD

Replace the *incorrect* word with the correct one (answers are at the back of the book):

1. To *affirm* [_____] means to allow or to permit something to be done or to happen.

2. The legal English word for compensation or money paid by the liable party to the successful party is *'interest'* [_____].

3. The term "under *pressure* [_____]" means that a person is being forced to do something that they do not want to do. In a legal English context it means that someone is forcing a party to sign or execute a contract that they do not want to sign

4. The legal English term that means two or more parties discuss their positions with a view to agreeing a settlement, agreement or a contract is to *accept* [_____]

5. There are three main types of *solution* [_____] in commercial contract disputes. The most common is damages, the second main type are equitable, such as an injunction or specific performance and the third main type are declaratory judgments.

6. The principle of the remedy called *restitution* [_____] is to put all the parties back in the position they were in before they entered into the contract.

7. Clause 3.5 of the contract states "the seller agrees to deliver the goods within 14 days of the date of the order *dependent* [_____] to full payment for all ordered goods having been received within 7 days of the date of the order".

8. Commercial contracts will usually state an exact date when payment must be made. This means that all *sums* [_____] owed by this date must be paid in full.

9. If the standard terms of a commercial contract do not vary, change or alter, then these provisions can be referred to as *original* [_____] provisions.

10. Once a contract is terminated and the parties are free of their contractual obligations, then it is said that the parties are *excused* [_____] from the contract.

11. An innominate term [_____] is a formal promise made that is intended to be relied upon. A commercial contract will contain a number of these, for instance, if the goods are defective then the seller will refund the buyer.

12. The document used to detail the products, goods or services that have been ordered by the buyer is called a *bill of lading* [_____].

13. Buyers and sellers must be aware of the potential *remedies* [_____]of entering into the contract. Accordingly, parties will include warranties, indemnities, guarantees and covenants.

14. Many commercial contracts need to be changed or altered at some point and so most agreements will include an *amendment* [_____] clause. This allows the parties to agree the terms of any changes in writing.

15. Examples of *restrictive covenants* [_____   _____] are force majeure, severability, governing law and jurisdiction clauses.

16. Clause 17.2 states "The contents of this agreement together with all supplementary documents will remain *exclusive* [_____] between the parties".

17. *Severability* [_____] clauses are very common in commercial contracts for goods because, for example, it provides the seller with certainty that the buyer will only sell the goods provided by the seller in a specific place.

18. The parties may wish to include a provision that restricts the amount of damages that can be claimed in the event of a breach contract. This type of clause is called an *exclusion* [_____] clause.

19. A clause, term or provision in the contract that is ruled unenforceable by the court and has no legal effect is called a *penalty* [_____] clause.

20. Civil litigation claims are also commonly called *disagreements* [_____].

8. ANSWERS

True or False:

1. True

2. False

3. True

4. False

5. True

6. False

7. True

8. True

9. True

10. False

11. True

12. False

13. True

14. False

15. True

16. False

17. True

18. True

19. False

20. True

Vocabulary Gap Fill:

1. agency

2. commerce

3. hire/rent

4. insurance

5. Subrogation

6. affirm

7. breach

8. Frustration

9. injunction

10. Privity

11. accrue

12. creditor

13. in arrears

14. time is of the essence

15. all reasonable endeavours

16. in default of

17. defective

18. liable

19. restrictive

20. warranty

Prepositions Gap Fill:

1. to

2. of

3. into

4. to

5. of

6. of

7. of

8. to

9. in/by

10. from

11. In

12. on

13. on/upon

14. under/at

15. for

16. from

17. in

18. of

19. to

20. to

Collocations Gap Fill:

1. credit

2. distribution

3. hire

4. goods

5. supply

6. take

7. unsolicited

8. Neither

9. set

10. art

11. lading

12. clear

13. tear

14. right

15. loan

16. added

17. give

18. restraint

19. off

20. purchase

Replace the Incorrect Word

1. ~~affirm~~, consent

2. ~~interest~~, damages

3. ~~pressure~~, duress

4. ~~accept~~, negotiate

5. ~~solution~~, remedy

6. ~~restitution~~, rescission

7. ~~dependent~~, subject

8. ~~owed~~, due

9. ~~original~~, default

10. ~~excused~~, discharged

11. ~~innominate term~~, guarantee

12. ~~bill of lading~~, invoice

13. ~~remedies~~, risks

14. ~~amendment~~, variation

15. ~~restrictive covenants~~, boilerplate clauses

16. ~~exclusive~~, confidential

17. ~~severability~~, exclusivity

18. ~~exclusion~~, limitation

19. ~~penalty~~, void

20. ~~disagreements~~, disputes

C. BUSINESS AND COMPANY LAW

1 BUSINESS STRUCTURES

Charity (noun): This type of business structure is a non-profiting making organisation. For a business structure to be classed as a charity it must conduct its business for the benefit of others without making a profit for itself. Charities are heavily regulated to ensure that they follow these principles. They must be registered and file information and accounts with the relevant authorities.

Associated Words: Accounts (noun), To File (verb), To Make a Profit (collocation), To Register (verb), To Regulate (verb).

Consortium (noun): This is a Latin word that means 'partnership'. It is used in legal English to describe a business arrangement that is similar in structure to a partnership. It is worth noting, however, that consortiums are commonly created to raise capital or equity for a specific purpose or event.

Associated Words: Capital (noun), Equity (noun), Partnership (noun), To Raise (verb).

Corporation (noun): A corporation is a state regulated organisation. Once a corporation is incorporated it becomes a separate legal entity. This means that it has its own legal personality and can sue and be sued. Corporations are subject to strict rules and regulations in relation to the way they are run and controlled. A corporation will usually be owned by its shareholders and run on a day-to-day basis by the directors.

Associated Words: Director (noun), To Incorporate (verb), Jurisdiction (noun), Legal Entity (noun), To Regulate (verb), To Run (verb), Shareholder (noun), To Sue (verb).

Enterprise (noun): This is a general English term for a business, organisation or firm that is involved in buying and selling goods or services

to consumers.
Associated Words: Consumer (noun), Goods (noun), To Trade (verb).

Joint Venture (noun): This is a business agreement or enterprise where parties co-operate for a specific purpose or project over a period of time. Joint ventures are commonly created in a similar way to partnerships but joint ventures usually end once the specific purpose or project has been completed. Parties to a joint venture will control decision-making in relation to management and financial issues. Types of joint ventures include joint ventures by limited guarantee, partnerships and consortiums.
Associated Words: Consortium (noun), Guarantee (noun), To Make a Profit (collocation).

Legal Entity (noun): This term means that an organisation or business is a separate legal person. A legal entity has its own legal personality and can issue proceedings or have proceedings issued against it. Common examples of separate legal entities are private limited companies and charities.
Associated Words: Charity (Noun), To Issue (verb), Private Limited Company (noun), Proceedings (noun).

Limited Liability Partnership (noun): This business structure is a type of partnership. The structure of a partnership means that the partners are personally liable for the debts of the partnership. If a partnership is a limited liability partnership, this means that the partners are only liable for the debts of the partnership up to a certain amount of money. Many law firms use this business structure and it is common to find the letters 'LLP' after the name of the law firm (the letters 'LLP' represent the words limited liability partnership).
Associated Words: Debt (noun), Liable (adjective), Partner (person).

Non-Governmental Organisation (noun): A non-governmental organisation (NGO) is a non-profit making organisation that is usually created for a specific social or charitable purpose. They are not run as conventional businesses or by the government or state. NGO's are usually run for a 'good cause' and many citizens help run them as paid employees or as volunteers.

Associated Words: Charitable (adjective), Employee (person), Profit (noun).

Off-The-Shelf Company (noun): This is an existing company that has been incorporated but is not actually in use. Off-the-shelf companies are available for individuals or other companies to start trading quickly, without needing to go through the incorporation process. The off-the-shelf-company's details can be changed immediately for the buyer. This means that the name, shareholders, directors and company secretary are all registered and set up easily and quickly. These types of business structures were more popular in the past because incorporating a company used to take a long time. However, now it is quicker to incorporate a company and, in some jurisdictions, a company can be incorporated online without the need to buy an off-the-shelf company.

Associated Words: Company Secretary (Person), Director (noun), To Incorporate (verb), Jurisdiction (noun), To Register (verb), Shareholder (noun).

Partnership (noun): This is a very common business structure. A partnership is a business owned by two or more people called 'Partners'. Each partner invests an amount of money into the partnership and, accordingly, owns a percentage of the business. The ownership and other important details are usually documented in a contract called a partnership agreement. A partnership is run and managed like a regular company, however, there is one very important difference between a partnership and a company. In a partnership, the partners are individually liable for the debts of the partnership.

Associated Words: Debt (noun), To Invest (verb), Liable (adjective), To Manage (verb), Partner (person), Partnership Agreement (noun).

Private Limited Company (noun): This type of business structure is a standard company structure. A private limited company is run by the directors and owned by its shareholders (also known as members or subscribers). It is 'limited' because the shareholders are only liable for the company's debts up to the amount of money that they invested in the company. Shares can only be bought in a private limited company with the company's permission. A private limited company is subject to more rules and regulations than a partnership and there are strict rules about filing company documentation and accounts. A company can appoint a company secretary to manage the filing of legal documents for the company.

Associated Words: To Appoint (verb), Debt (noun), Director (noun), To File Documents (collocation), To Guarantee (verb), To Invest (verb), Liable (adjective), Partnership (noun), Shareholder (noun), Shares (noun).

Public Limited Company (noun): A public limited company (also known as a 'PLC') is a business structure similar to a private limited company. The company is owned by its shareholders and run and managed by the directors. The main difference between a PLC and a private limited company is that the shares of the company may be bought and sold freely on a stock exchange. PLCs generally have far more shareholders and directors than a private limited company. Due to the fact that PLCs are larger businesses, they are subject to extremely strict rules and regulations, including rules on buying and selling shares of the company.

Associated Words: Director (noun), Shareholder (noun), Shares (noun).

Self-employed (adjective): This means that a person works individually without formally incorporating as a company or registering as an employee. The structure is also known as a sole-trader. This is a less formal type of business structure, but it is still subject to strict tax rules and regulations. The individual is responsible for filing all tax information with the correct tax authority and to calculate the amount of tax owed (if any). This is the easiest and most basic structure of working as a business. However, a self-employed individual is liable for all of the debts incurred because it does not benefit from any type of limited liability.

Associated Words: Debt (noun), Employee (person), To File (verb), To Incorporate (verb), To Incur Debt (collocation), Liable (adjective), Partnership (noun), Sole-Trader (person).

2 SETTING UP A BUSINESS

Articles of Association (noun): Every registered company must have their own articles of association. The articles of association (also known simply as 'articles') set out the responsibilities, rules and regulations of the management of the company. These articles will define what the company can do, the roles and duties of the directors and the extent of the powers of the shareholders. It is the main, fundamental document for a registered company. There is a template version of the articles of association, which is commonly used by companies with simple structures. The articles of association, the memorandum of association and the certificate of incorporation make up the constitution of a standard company.
Associated Words: Certificate of Incorporation (noun), Director (noun), Memorandum of Association (noun), Shareholder (noun).

To Acquire (verb): This verb means to get or obtain something. In the language of business and company law it is used to describe a person or organisation buying shares or a business. The noun 'acquisition' is found in the corporate law practice area of mergers and acquisitions.
Associated Words: Acquired (past simple), Acquired (3rd form), Merger (noun), Shares (noun).

Certificate of Incorporation (noun): This is the official document that states a company is legally established and all relevant documentation has been filed with the relevant authorities. Once a company has filed all the correct information, the certificate will be sent to the registered office of the company and the company will be issued with a company number.
Associated Words: Companies House (noun), To File (verb).

To Contribute To (collocation): This means to give or provide something in order to achieve something. In business and company law, partners contribute capital to the partnership in order to receive a percentage of the profits.
Associated Words: Contributed To (past simple), Contributed To (3rd form), Capital (noun), Partner (person), Partnership (noun), Profit (noun).

To Draw Up (phrasal verb): This phrasal verb is used when creating an agreement or contract and means to create or draft. For instance, when a partnership is created it is common for the parties to 'draw up' a partnership agreement to set out the important details including the ownership proportions.

Associated Words: Drew Up (past simple), Drawn Up (3rd form), Partnership Agreement (noun).

To Go Into Business With (collocation): This collocation means to co-operate or collaborate. It is commonly used when business partners enter into a type of enterprise together or for two or more businesses entering into a type of business deal or venture.

Associated Words: Went Into Business With (past simple), Gone Into Business With (3rd form), Enterprise (noun), Venture (noun).

To Incorporate (verb): This verb is used in legal English to describe the process of formally establishing a company and successfully registering it with the relevant authorities. To incorporate a company, certain information must be filed including the name of the company, registered office, share capital, shareholders and directors. Upon incorporation, the company is sent a certificate of incorporation confirming the completion of the incorporation process.

Associated Words: Incorporated (past simple), Incorporated (3rd form), Certificate of Incorporation (noun), Director (noun), To File (verb), Share Capital (noun), Shareholder (noun).

To Invest In (phrasal verb): This phrasal verb is used when an individual or organisation (an 'investor') puts money into a business. A common way for investors to invest in businesses is to buy shares in a company. The investors will then wait for a return on their investment, which can be by way of a dividend or selling their shares at a higher price than when they bought them.

Associated Words: Invested In (past simple), Invested in (3rd form), Investor (noun/person), Investment (noun), Dividend (noun), Return (noun), Shares (noun), To Issue Shares (collocation).

To Issue Shares (collocation): To issues shares means to distribute or transfer shares in a company to an investor or shareholder. For example, Company ABC issues 200 shares of £1 each to 4 individual shareholders. The issued share capital of the company is £200. Another way of saying to issue shares is to 'allot shares'.

Associated Words: Issued Shares (past simple), Issued Shares (3rd form), Issued Share Capital (noun), To Incorporate (verb), Shares (noun), Shareholder (noun).

Issued Share Capital (noun): This is the number of shares that the company has issued in total to shareholders at the nominal amount. It is important to remember that the issued share capital is not the value of the shares. For instance, if a company has issued 100 shares at £1 each, the issued share capital is £100. The value of these shares may be higher or lower depending on the performance of the company. Usually, there will be a difference between the issued share capital and the actual value of the shares.

Associated Words: To Issue Shares (collocation), Nominal Value (noun).

To List (verb): This verb is used when a company wishes to be placed on a public stock exchange. In business and company legal English public limited companies are 'listed' on a stock exchange. Another way to say this is that the company has 'floated'.

Associated Words: Listed (past simple), Listed (3rd form), Public Limited Company (noun), Stock Exchange (noun).

Memorandum of Association (noun): This is a formal document that states the basic information of the company. A company must have a memorandum of association to be incorporated. It is one of the most important documents, together with the articles of association and the certificate of incorporation. A new company needs these three documents to register with the relevant authorities. These requirements and documents will differ in different jurisdictions.

Associated Words: Articles of Association (noun), Certificate of Incorporation (noun), To Incorporate (verb), To Register (verb).

To Merge With (phrasal verb): This phrasal verb is commonly used in business and legal English to describe the act of two companies joining together to create one business or entity. For example, it is common for US law firms to merge with law firms from other parts of the world to help grow their business globally.
Associated Words: Merged With (past simple), Merged With (3rd form), Merger (noun), Company (noun), Entity (noun).

Nominal Value (noun): This means the original value of a share in a company. When a company is incorporated it has one or more shares at a set value. This is called the 'nominal value'. The actual value of the share or shares will change depending on the performance of the company.
Associated Words: Company (noun), To Incorporate (verb), Shares (noun).

Partnership Agreement (noun): This is a formal document stating the terms upon which the partners agree to own and manage the partnership. A partnership agreement will usually deal with issues including the name of the partnership, the ownership proportions of each partner, and the drawings of each party.
Associated Words: Partner (person), Drawings (noun).

To Raise Finance (collocation): This collocation means to find or produce an amount of money or capital. The phrase is used in business English in relation to fund a specific project, to sell shares in a company or to use other financial instruments to obtain an amount of money required for a specific purpose.
Associated Words: Raised Finance (past simple), Raised Finance (3rd form), Capital (noun), Shares (noun).

To Register (verb): This verb means to apply to be a member of an organisation or club. In business legal English, it is used for businesses and other entities to apply or join the list of incorporated companies at a company registrar. It is common for formal paperwork and documentation to be completed and a fee paid for a company to be registered.
Associated Words: Registered (past simple), Registered (3rd form), Company (noun), To Incorporate (verb).

Registered Office (noun): This is the legal English term for the official address of a company. Every company must have a registered office as all legal and formal documentation is sent to the registered address by the company registrar and other authorities.
Associated Words: Company (noun), Company Registrar (noun).

To Set Up (phrasal verb): To set up a company means to establish or form a company. It is an informal phrase but commonly used in legal and business English.
Associated Words: Set Up (past simple), Set Up (3rd form), Company (noun).

Share Capital (noun): This means the total amount of the nominal value of all of the shares issued by a company. For example, a new company called LEB Ltd is set up. Upon incorporation, it issued 1,000 shares at £1 each. Recently it issued 500 more shares, also at £1 each. The total share capital of LEB Ltd is now £1,500.
Associated Words: Company (noun), To Incorporate (verb), To Issue Shares (collocation), Nominal Value (noun), To Set Up (phrasal verb), Shares (noun).

Shares/Stocks (noun): A share is a unit or part of a company. The term is used to express how the capital of a company is owned. The owners of the shares are called shareholders (or stockholders). Each shareholder will have a share certificate that states how many shares they own. Shareholders have the right to vote on important decisions about the company. The value of their shares will change depending on the performance of the company.
Associated Words: Company (noun), Share Certificate (noun), Shareholder/Stockholder (noun).

Stock Exchange (noun): This is an organisation that buys and sells stocks and shares, also known as trading. Only public limited companies (not private limited companies) can trade on a stock exchange. There are very strict rules and regulations on the procedure of buying and selling shares. Usually, a trained professional known as a stockbroker will trade on behalf of the buyer or seller. If a company wishes to trade their shares on a stock exchange then it must apply to be 'listed'. The procedure of applying to be listed on a stock exchange is also known as 'floatation'.

Associated Words: To List (verb), Private Limited Company (noun), Public Limited Company (noun), Shares (noun), Stockbroker (person).

Takeover (noun): In business English this word describes the situation when a company takes control or acquires another company, usually by purchasing a majority shareholding. A company that is being bought is called the 'Target'. The buyer is called the 'Acquirer' or 'Bidder'. There are a number of different types of shareholding, including a friendly takeover where the board of directors accepts the takeover, a hostile takeover where the board do not want to be taken over and a reverse takeover where a private company acquires a public limited company.

Associated Words: To Takeover (verb), To Acquire (verb), Board of Directors (noun), Company (noun), Private Limited Company (noun), Public Limited Company (noun).

To Trade (verb): In business and legal English this verb means to buy or sell goods or services.

Associated Words: Traded (past simple), Traded (3rd form).

To Trade Under (collocation): This collocation is used in relation to the name of a company or business that is used as the brand name. For example, a company may be incorporated under the name 'ABC Legal English Books Systems XYZ Ltd' but it may choose to trade under the shorter and simpler name of 'Legal English Books'. It is common for a company to be incorporated under one name and to trade under another.

Associated Words: Traded Under (past simple), Traded Under (3rd form), Company (noun), To Incorporate (verb).

3 PEOPLE IN BUSINESS

Accountant (person): This is a person, or a firm, who keeps and examines financial records of a company or other organisation.
Associated Words: Accountancy (noun), Company (noun), To Owe (verb).

Administrator (person): An administrator manages the insolvency procedure known called administration. The administrator attempts to rescue insolvent entities and allow them to carry on running their business. This is also referred to as the business trading as a 'going concern'. The administrator must act in the interests of all the creditors and attempt to rescue the company. If the rescue attempt fails, the administrator recovers as much of the creditors' money as possible.
Associated Words: Administration (noun), Company (noun), Creditor (noun), Insolvent (Adjective).

Auditor (person): An auditor is a person from an external company, for example, an accountancy firm, who investigate and examine a company's accounts and documentation to check that the company is being run in accordance with all rules and regulations.
Associated Words: Company (noun), To Run (verb).

Board (noun): The board of the company, also known as the board of directors, is the executive function of the company. The most important decisions of the company are made by the board of directors. Usually, each member of the board will have his or her own specific area to manage. For instance, a standard board of directors includes a managing director, finance director, marketing director, etc.
Associated Words: Company (noun), Executive (noun).

Chairperson (person): This person leads, or 'chairs', the board and company meetings. This means that they set the agenda of the meeting and control the structure and schedule of who speaks. The chairperson also holds the 'casting vote'. This means that if a vote on a motion is equal for both yes and no votes, the chairperson has the final vote on whether the motion is

passed or not.
Associated Words: Board (noun), Company (noun), Motion (noun).

Company Secretary (noun): This person performs an administrative function for the company. A company secretary is responsible for filing all relevant legal documentation with the authorities, for example, annual returns and share registers. Smaller sized companies may not need to have a company secretary but most companies will have a similar role in the organisation.
Associated Words: Annual Return (noun), Company (noun), To File (verb).

Creditor (noun): This is a person or organisation that is owed money. The easiest way to remember what a creditor is, is that they are 'in credit'. For instance, if a company needs a loan to pay for new equipment then they may go to a bank. If the bank agree to lend the company money, then the bank is the creditor. The company is called the debtor in this situation. **Associated Words:** Company (noun), Debtor (noun), Loan (noun), To Owe (verb).

Debtor (noun): This is a person or organisation that owes money to someone. For instance, if a law firm needs to finance a new building for their employees, then they will apply for a loan from the bank. In this scenario, the law firm is the debtor and the bank is the creditor.
Associated Words: Creditor (noun), Employee (person), Loan (noun), To Owe (verb).

Director (noun): A director is a person who has a formal, decision-making position in the company. A director does not have to be an employee of the company but, importantly, they owe a fiduciary duty to act in the best interests of the company when they make decisions. Accordingly, there are rules and regulations that come with the responsibility of being a director. There are three main types of directors. An executive director is involved in day-to-day decision making, a non-executive director assists with specific issues rather than day-to-day management and a shadow director supports the company on an informal advisory basis.
Associated Words: Company (noun), Fiduciary Duty (noun).

Dormant Partner (person): This person will invest or contribute to a partnership. Commonly, this is a financial investment or contribution. A dormant partner is not involved in the day to day running of the partnership but receives a proportional share of any profits.
Associated Words: To Contribute (verb), Equity Partner (person), Loss (noun), Partnership (noun), Profit (noun), Salaried Partner (person).

Employee (person): An employee is a general word for a person who has an employment contract with a company, firm or organisation to provide services in return for remuneration. There are important rights given to employees in relation to working conditions, hours, annual leave, sick pay, pensions and overtime. A company, firm or organisation that employs an employee is called an employer.
Associated Words: Annual Leave (noun), Company (noun), Employer (noun), Overtime (noun), Pension (noun), Remuneration (noun), Sick Pay (noun).

Employer (noun): An employer is a company, firm or organisation that employs a person or people to provide services pursuant to a contract of employment. There are strict regulatory provisions for employers to follow in relation to the treatment of its employees.
Associated Words: Company (noun), Employee (person).

Equity Partner (person): This type of partner receives a proportional share of the partnership profits as their remuneration. These are called drawings. An equity partner owns a percentage of the partnership and will have an agreement with the partnership for how much and how often they may withdraw their remuneration in drawings. They will also be liable for the same proportion should the partnership make a loss.
Associated Words: Drawings (noun), Loss (noun), Partnership (noun), Profit (noun), Remuneration (noun).

Executive Director (person): This is a position on the board of a company. An executive director is involved in the main day-to-day running and decision making of the company. Usually, executive directors will have different specific roles to cover the main aspects of managing a company.

Associated Words: Board (noun), Company (noun).

Founder (Noun): This means a person who started a company, firm or organisation. The word founder derives from the verb to found, which means to begin or establish. A founder or founders of a company usually hold subscriber shares in the company.
Associated Words: Company (noun), To Establish (verb).

Insolvency Practitioner (noun): This is a person who undertakes formal insolvency proceedings. All formal insolvency proceedings should be carried out by a licensed insolvency practitioner. A licensed insolvency practitioner has authority to conduct insolvency proceedings such as administration, bankruptcy proceedings, liquidation and voluntary arrangements.
Associated Words: Insolvency (noun), Administration (noun), Bankruptcy (noun), Liquidation (noun).

Liquidator (noun): This is a type of insolvency practitioner who is appointed to liquidate the company. To liquidate the company means to formally close it. This is also known as 'winding up' the company. The job of the liquidator is to realise the assets of the company. To realise the assets means to sell the assets of the company and to distribute the proceeds to the creditors of the company.
Associated Words: To Liquidate (verb), Liquidation (noun), Assets (noun), Company (noun), Creditor (noun), To Realise (verb), To Wind Up (Phrasal Verb).

Member (noun): A member of a company is another name for a shareholder of a company.
Associated Words: Company (noun), Shareholder (noun).

Non-Executive Director (person): This is a type of director who is not involved in the day-to-day running of a company. The role of a non-executive director is to advise on specific matters upon which the company requires expert knowledge. For example, a non-executive director may be used when the company requires knowledge on issues such as technology or product design.

Associated Words: Director (person), Company (noun).

Official Receiver (noun): An official receiver is an officer of the insolvency services. Their duty is to the court. They act as a receiver, trustee or liquidator in insolvency proceedings. The official receiver will examine a company's financial records, make background enquiries and report back to creditors and shareholders of the company. Their main role is to sell the assets of the company and distribute the proceeds to the creditors.
Associated Words: Receivership (noun), Assets (noun), Company (noun), Creditor (noun), To Examine (verb), Insolvency (noun), Liquidator (noun), Shareholder (noun), Trustee (noun).

Partner (noun): In legal English a partner is a party to an agreement to co-operate with other partners for the achievement of their mutual interests or targets. This is collectively known as a partnership. Partners may form a partnership on a formal or informal basis. Commonly, partners will enter into a partnership agreement in order for their rights and liabilities to be set out in writing. A partner will usually have the right to a proportion of any profit made by the partnership, or conversely will be liable for a proportion of any loss.
Associated Words: Partnership (noun), Loss (noun), Profit (noun).

Proxy (noun): This is a person who can vote on a motion in a company or board meeting on behalf of a shareholder or board member who is not able to attend. The absent voter votes by proxy and will instruct someone they trust to attend the meeting and represent their vote.
Associated Words: To Vote By Proxy (collocation), Board Meeting (noun), Company Meeting (noun), Shareholder (noun).

To Resign (verb): This verb describes the situation where a director, partner or employee gives notice to the company or firm that they are terminating their employment contract.
Associated Words: Resigned (past simple), Resigned (3rd form), Resignation (noun), Company (noun), Director (noun), Employee (person), Notice Period (noun), Partner (person), To Terminate (verb).

To Retire (verb): This means a person has decided to end their working career. It is common for employees to work until a minimum age, for example 65 years old, and then retire. Upon retirement they usually receive a pension. A pension is a salary paid to people who are retired.
Associated Words: Retired (past simple), Retired (3rd form), Retirement (noun), Employee (person), Pension (noun).

Salaried Partner (person): A salaried partner is a member of the partnership who receives their remuneration by way of a salary rather than by way of drawings.
Associated Words: Drawings (noun), Partnership (noun), Remuneration (noun).

Service Agreement (noun): This is an agreement a director enters into that states their role, position and duties. A director of a company has different roles in a company than that of an employee and a service agreement helps to state clearly what the directors' responsibilities are.
Associated Words: Company (noun), Director (noun).

Shadow Director (person): This is not an official director of a company, however, a shadow director offers the executive and non-executive directors advice and expertise on specific issues. The executive and non-executive directors usually seek such advice as shadow directors are used for particular purposes and in particular business situations.
Associated Words: Company (noun), Director (noun), Executive Director (noun), Non-Executive Director (noun), Shareholder (noun).

Shareholder (noun): A shareholder is a person or institution that owns a share (also known as stock) of a company. The number of shares they own represents the proportion of the company they own. The shareholder can then use this shareholding to vote on important matters in relation to the way the company is run and managed. Shares will have certain rights attached to them and so different shareholders may have different types of shares. Shareholders own both private limited companies and public limited companies. Another name for shareholders is members.
Associated Words: Shares (noun), Member (noun), Private Limited

Company (noun), Public Limited Company (noun), Rights (noun).

Sleeping Partner (person): A sleeping partner is also known as a silent partner or a dormant partner. A sleeping partner contributes to the partnership but is not involved in the day-to-day running of the partnership. This contribution is usually by way of financial investment. Due to the contributions, this partner will still receive a share of the partnership profits. **Associated Words:** Silent Partner (noun), Dormant Partner (noun), Partnership (noun), Profit (noun).

Stockbroker (person): This is a person who buys and sells stocks and shares on the stock market or stock exchange. A stockbroker is heavily regulated by law and there are strict rules that state when shares can be bought or sold. A stockbroker acts as an agent for their clients and will charge a fee or commission for the transactions. **Associated Words:** Agent (noun), To Charge (verb), Commission (noun), Fee (noun), Shares (noun), Stock (noun), Stock Exchange (noun), Stock Market (noun).

4 RUNNING A BUSINESS

Accounts (noun): The accounts of a company or organisation are records of all the financial transactions in any one financial year. All businesses must keep accurate accounts of their business transactions. This means that a detailed written record must be kept in order for the tax authorities and the company registrar to see that they are following legal business practice and paying the correct amount of tax. A company may have specialist accounting employees to assist with this task, but most will employ external accountants or auditors to examine the business transactions and to make sure they comply with all relevant legislation.
Associated Words: Accountant (person), Auditor (person), To Comply With (phrasal verb), Employee (person), Registrar (noun), Tax (noun).

Annual Return (noun): This is a formal document that a company must complete and send to the company registrar every year. The document is used for a company to update its details in relation to directors, shareholders, accounts and other information. It is an obligatory document and there are strict fines for late or non-delivery of annual returns.
Associated Words: Accounts (noun), Director (noun), Registrar (noun), Shareholder (noun).

Assets (noun): The idea of an asset can be rather complicated but in business and legal English it is usually used to describe something that a person or institution owns that has value. An asset can be a physical thing, for example property, but it can also be something that you cannot touch, for instance, a good reputation.

Authorised Share Capital (noun): This means the maximum amount of share capital that a company is allowed to issue to shareholders. This amount is set out in the constitutional documents of the company, for instance, the articles of association. Note that it does not mean the amount of shares that have been issued or allotted. The amount of share capital that has been sold or allotted to shareholders is called the issued share capital.
Associated Words: Issued Share Capital (noun), To Allot Shares

(collocation), Articles of Association (noun), Company (noun), To Issue Shares (collocation).

Balance sheet (noun): This is a 'snapshot' of a company's finances at any given point in time. A standard balance sheet will show the total liabilities of the company and the total assets of the company.
Associated Words: Assets (noun), Company (noun), Liabilities (noun).

To Close a Deal (collocation): This means to complete a deal or other type of business transaction.
Associated Words: Closed a Deal (past simple), Closed a Deal (3rd form).

Conflict of Interest (collocation): This means that an individual or organisation has two or more beneficial interests in a situation or business transaction. A common example of this is with directors. Directors have a fiduciary duty to act in the best interests of the company. If a director has a personal interest that conflicts with this fiduciary duty, then there is a conflict of interest and this must be disclosed by the director to the company.
Associated Words: Director (noun), Fiduciary Duty (noun).

Corporation Tax (noun): This is a tax paid by companies and other organisations on any profits they make.
Associated Words: Company (noun), Profit (noun).

To Declare a Dividend (collocation): This collocation is used when a company officially announces whether or not a dividend is to be paid to its shareholders, and if so, how much. A dividend is a payment to shareholders, usually annually. A dividend is calculated as a fixed price per share with members receiving an amount of money in proportion to their shareholding.
Associated Words: Declared a Dividend (past simple), Declared a Dividend (3rd form), Annual (adjective), Company (noun), Dividend, Member (noun), Shares (noun).

To Disclose Information (collocation): To disclose information means to send or show information to a relevant person on a formal basis. In business and company law, the verb to disclose relates to an open disclosure of information. It is common for directors to have to disclose all information to the company if they believe they are subject to a conflict of interest in a business situation or deal.

Associated Words: Disclosed Information (past simple), Disclosed Information (3rd form), Company (noun), Conflict of Interest (collocation), Director (noun).

To Draw (verb): This verb is used in relation to partners and remuneration. Some partners, especially equity partners, will receive their remuneration by way of drawings. To draw money means that they will receive an agreed amount of money, usually every month, and this money is treated as their salary or remuneration.

Associated Words: Drew (past simple), Drew (3rd form), Drawings (noun), Equity Partner (person), Remuneration (noun).

Expenses (noun): This means the costs incurred by company employees and directors in the course of their business. For instance, common expenses are travelling costs and hotels for business trips. The company will usually reimburse expenses claimed by employees and directors if they were incurred in the course of business.

Associated Words: Company (noun), Director (noun), Employee (person).

Fiduciary Duty (noun): In business and company law this phrase is usually used in relation to a director owing a fiduciary duty to their company. A fiduciary duty means that a director must act in the best interests of the company, to act in good faith at all times and declare any conflicts of interest.

Associated Words: Company (noun), Conflict of Interest (collocation), Good Faith (collocation).

To Fluctuate (verb): In business legal English this verb means to change value or price. The verb to fluctuate is commonly used with share prices to describe the movement of the price rising or falling.

Associated Words: Fluctuated (past simple), Fluctuated (3rd form), Shares (noun).

To Hold/Own Shares (phrasal verb): To hold or to own shares means to possess or have shares in a company. An individual or organisation can buy shares in a public limited company, or a private limited company if approved by the shareholders.
Associated Words: Held/Owned Shares (past simple), Held/Owned Shares (3rd form), Company (noun), Private Limited Company (noun), Public Limited Company (noun), Shares (noun).

Income Tax (noun): This is a tax that an employee, contractor or any other worker pays on the income they receive.
Associated Words: Employee (person), Income (noun).

To Invest (verb): This verb is used in business and company law with the purchase of shares or other equipment to be used to improve the business. When an individual or organisation buys shares in a company, it is also known as investing. However, investments can also include purchasing premises, employing staff or buying equipment.
Associated Words: Invested (past simple), Invested (3rd form), Investment (noun), Company (noun), Shares (noun), Premises (noun).

Invoice (noun): This is a document that states the goods or services that have been bought in a transaction and how much they cost.
Associated Words: To Invoice (verb), Goods (noun).

Joint and Several Liability (collocation): This phrase means that if there is a group of two or more people who are liable for a debt, then all of the members of the group are liable individually and also together as a group. For example, if Mr and Mrs Benson are liable for damages, the court may order that the liability is joint and several. This means that Mr Smith is liable for all of the debt, Mrs Smith is liable for all the debt, and together Mr and Mrs Smith are liable for the debt. The court can enforce the judgment against both Mr and Mrs Benson individually or together.
Associated Words: Damages (noun), To Enforce (verb), Liable (noun), To Order (verb).

To Lay Off (phrasal verb): This is an informal phrase that means to make redundant, to sack or to fire an employee.
Associated Words: Laid Off (past simple), Laid Off (3rd form), Employee (person), To Make Redundant (collocation).

Liable (adjective): This means that a party is legally responsible for their actions or omissions. Omissions means that a party did not do something that they should have done. If a party is liable then the court will usually order the liable party to remedy the damage or problem. This can be with money, known as damages, or action, known as an injunction.
Associated Words: Damages (noun), Injunction (noun), Party (noun).

Limited Liability (collocation): This means that a shareholder's liability is limited to the amount of shares that they hold in a company. If a company enters insolvency proceedings, a shareholder is not liable for any debt over the amount of their shareholding.
Associated Words: Company (noun), Debt (noun), To Hold Shares (collocation), Insolvency Proceedings (noun), Shares (noun).

To Make a Loss (collocation): To make a loss means that a company or other organisation has spent more money than they have received. Commonly, this means that the costs of running the business are higher than the revenue received.
Associated Words: Made a Loss (past simple), Made a Loss (3rd form), Revenue (noun), To Run a Business (collocation).

To Make Redundant (collocation): This phrase is used when a company decides to re-structure the work force and reduce the number of their employees. There are strict procedures for making an employee redundant.
Associated Words: Made Redundant (past simple), Made Redundant (3rd form), Company (noun), Employee (person).

To Manage (verb): To manage (or run) a business means to control and organise the business.
Associated Words: Managed (past simple), Managed (3rd form).

Market Value (noun): This means the standard or normal cost of goods or services. The market value of a good or service is the normal price that a reasonable person would pay for that good or service.
Associated Words: Goods (noun), Service (noun).

Notice (noun): This means stating or notifying that something has been done or a party wishes to do something. Notice provisions in a contract usually relate to specific information that must be given to another party. For example, some commercial contracts can be terminated upon notice. This means that one party states to the other that they wish to end the contract. There will usually be a notice period for this event, for example, a contract may state that the notice period for terminating the contract is four weeks. This is called giving notice.
Associated Words: To Give Notice (collocation), Notice Period (noun), Provision (noun), To Terminate (verb).

Profit (noun): This means that a company or other institution receives more revenue than they spend on costs and expenses.
Associated Words: Company (noun), Expenses (noun), Revenue (noun).

Profit and Loss Account (noun): This is a financial document that shows the income and expenses of a business for a financial year.
Associated Words: Income (noun), Expense (noun).

Regulations (noun): This is a generic word in legal English that means rules, laws or policies.

Return on Investment (collocation): In business and company law, a return on investment usually means the profit made on an investment. For example, it is common for individuals or institutions to buy shares in public limited company and then to sell those shares later at a higher price. The profit made on the sale of the shares is also known as a return on the investment.
Associated Words: Company (noun), Investment (noun), Profit (noun), Public Limited Company (noun), Shares (noun).

To Run a Business (collocation): This is a common collocation that means to organise and manage a business on a day-to-day basis.

Associated Words: Ran a Business (past simple), Run a Business (3rd form), To Manage (verb).

To Subscribe to Shares (collocation): To subscribe to shares means to buy shares in a private or public company. A person or institution that subscribes to shares is also known as a member or shareholder.

Associated Words: Subscribed to Shares (past simple), Subscribed to Shares (3rd form), Private Limited Company (noun), Public Limited Company (noun), Shares (noun).

5 BUSINESS MEETINGS

To Adjourn (verb): This verb is used in business and company law to describe the process of stopping a meeting with the intention of re-starting the meeting at a later date or time.
Associated Words: Adjourned (past simple), Adjourned (3rd Form).

Agenda (noun): An agenda is a formal plan for a company or board meeting. Most companies will have an agenda, set by the chairperson and circulated before the meeting begins. The agenda lists all the items for discussion with any action points to be completed.
Associated Words: Board Meeting (noun), Chairperson (person), Company Meeting (noun).

Annual General Meeting 'AGM' (noun): An annual general meeting is a company meeting of company shareholders held once a year. The meeting is seen to be one of the most important meetings in the calendar year. Shareholders will discuss the most important aspects of company management, financial results, the directors and whether a dividend is paid.
Associated Words: Company (noun), Director (noun), Dividend (noun), Shareholder (noun).

To Appoint (verb): To appoint means to officially state that a person has been accepted into a position or role. For example, in business and company law the verb to appoint can be used when a director is appointed to the board of a company.
Associated Words: Appointed (past simple), Appointed (3rd form), Board (noun), Director (noun).

Board Meeting (noun): This is a meeting convened for the board of directors to discuss and vote on running and managing the business on a day-to-day basis. The most senior director, who also holds the casting vote, chairs board meetings.
Associated Words: Casting Vote (noun), Director (noun).

To Carry a Motion (collocation): This means that a motion or proposal in a company or board meeting is passed and approved by way of a vote.
Associated Words: Motion Carried (collocation in the past tense), Board Meeting (noun), Company Meeting (noun).

To Chair a Meeting (collocation): To chair a meeting means to organize or manage the structure and agenda of a company or board meeting. The person who chairs a meeting is called a chairperson and usually holds the casting vote in the event of a tie between the other attendees.
Associated Words: Chaired a Meeting (past simple), Chaired a Meeting (3rd form), Agenda (noun), Board Meeting (noun), Casting Vote (noun), Company Meeting (noun).

Company Meeting (noun): This is a meeting for the shareholders of a company. Appropriate notice must be given to all shareholders who have the right to attend such meetings. These meetings are used to propose motions, vote and pass any resolutions that the shareholders see fit.
Associated Words: Company (noun), Motion (noun), To Pass a Resolution (collocation), Rights (noun), Shareholders (noun), To Vote (verb).

To Convene (verb): This verb is used in business and company law to describe the act of organising a company or board meeting. For example, *'The next board meeting has been convened to take place on 24th February'*.
Associated Words: Convened (past simple), Convened (3rd form), Board Meeting (noun), Company Meeting (noun).

To Declare (verb): The most common use for this verb in business and company law is when a company declares a dividend to be paid to the shareholders. A dividend is usually declared annually.
Associated Words: Declared (past simple) Declared (3rd form), Company (noun), Dividend (noun), Shareholder (noun).

To Draw Attention To (collocation): This is a formal phrase that means to suggest a colleague or client looks at a certain document or piece of information. It is common in board and company meetings for individuals to draw attention to documents, financial figures or aspects of management that are important to the business. For example, *'May I draw everyone's attention to item 3 on the agenda'*.

Associated Words: Drew Attention To (past simple), Drew Attention To (3rd form), Agenda (noun), Board Meeting (noun), Company Meeting (noun).

To Elect (verb): To elect means to vote on a situation and to approve the result of the vote. For instance, it is common for shareholders and directors to vote and elect certain positions in a company, for example a managing director.

Associated Words: Elected (past simple), Elected (3rd form), Company (noun), Director (noun), Shareholder (noun).

To Exercise (a right or power) (collocation): To exercise a right or a power is commonly used with voting rights in company and board meetings. For instance, shareholders or directors can exercise their right to vote, exercise their right to abstain from voting or exercise their right to vote by proxy. To exercise a right or power means to use that right or power.

Associated Words: Exercised (past simple), Exercised (3rd form), To Abstain (verb), Board Meeting (noun), Company Meeting (noun), Director (noun), Shareholder (noun).

To Expel (verb): To expel a person means to remove them from office or their position in a partnership. It is usually a condition in the partnership agreement that collectively the partners have the right to expel a partner under certain circumstances.

Associated Words: Expelled (past simple), Expelled (3rd form), Partner (person), Partnership (noun), Partnership Agreement (noun).

Extraordinary General Meeting 'EGM' (noun): An extraordinary general meeting ('EGM') is a meeting convened for the shareholders to discuss and vote on matters that are seen as too important to wait for the annual general meeting. For example, if the company wishes to increase their authorised share capital, change their name or pay an interim dividend, then it is likely that an EGM will be called for these types of issues to be discussed.

Associated Words: Annual General Meeting (noun), Company (noun), To Convene (verb), Dividend (noun), Authorised Share Capital (noun).

Majority (noun): In business and company law the term majority is used in relation to voting at company and board meetings. A majority vote is when more than half of the total votes are cast in favour of a proposal or motion. For instance, an ordinary resolution requires a majority vote for it to be passed. This means that 50% plus 1 vote is needed for the ordinary resolution to be passed.

Associated Words: Board Meeting (noun), Company Meeting (noun), Minority (noun), Motion (noun), Ordinary Resolution (noun), To Pass a Resolution (collocation).

Minority (noun): A minority has the opposite meaning of 'majority'. It means that less than 50% of the total votes were cast for a proposal or motion. In business and company law, a minority vote is not enough to pass an ordinary resolution. For example, if 49% vote in favour of a motion, the motion will not be passed.

Associated Words: Majority (noun), Motion (noun), Ordinary Resolution (noun), To Pass a Resolution (noun).

Minutes (noun): Minutes are the written record of what is said and voted on in company and board meetings.

Associated Words: Board Meeting (noun), Company Meeting (noun).

Motion (noun): A motion is a formal legal English term that means proposal. In company and board meetings, attendees may put forward motions that believe will be beneficial to the running of the business. The attendees will then vote on these motions. If successful, the motion is passed as a resolution.

Associated Words: Board Meeting (noun), Company Meeting (noun), To Pass a Resolution.

To Obtain a Majority (collocation): This means to achieve enough 'Yes' votes for a motion to pass and become a resolution in a board or company meeting. A simple majority in this case will be a total of 50% plus one vote or more. To obtain means to get or receive in this context.

Associated Words: Obtained a Majority (past simple), Obtained a Majority (3rd form), Board Meeting (noun), Company Meeting (noun), Motion (noun), To Pass a Resolution (collocation).

Ordinary Resolution (noun): An ordinary resolution is a proposal or motion that has been successfully voted on by 50% plus 1 vote or more of the meeting's attendees. This means that the motion becomes a resolution. For example, a director of XYZ Ltd puts a motion on the agenda of a company meeting for a new pension scheme to be adopted by the company. The resolution that is required is an ordinary resolution. This is stated in the company's articles of association. The attendees of the meeting vote on the motion and after counting all the votes, 66% of the attendees vote in favour. This means that the ordinary resolution to change the pension scheme has been passed.
Associated Words: Special Resolution (noun), Agenda (noun), Articles of Association (noun), Board Meeting (noun), Company Meeting (noun), Motion.

To Pass a Resolution (collocation): This means a motion or proposal receives enough votes for it to be approved. The number of votes that a motion needs depends on whether a resolution is an ordinary resolution or a special resolution.
Associated Words: Passed a Resolution (past simple), Passed a Resolution (3rd form), Motion (noun), Ordinary Resolution (noun), Special Resolution (noun).

Poll (noun): In business and legal English, a poll is a vote either by way of individuals (a show of hands) or by percentage of shares held.
Associated Word: Shares (noun).

To Propose (verb): This verb is a formal way to suggest something. In business English, motions are proposed, then discussed and voted on in board and company meetings.
Associated Words: Proposed (past simple), Proposed (3rd form), Board Meeting (noun), Company Meeting (noun), Motion (noun).

Quorum (noun): A quorum is the smallest number of people that need to be present at a company or board meeting before it can officially begin and

before official decisions can be made. If there are enough attendees for a meeting who have the right to vote, it is said that the meeting is 'quorate'.
Associated Words: Board Meeting (noun), Company Meeting (noun).

Resolution (noun): A resolution is a motion that has been voted on and passed by the attendees of the company or board meeting. Resolutions are ideas or proposals that are set on the meeting agenda usually in relation to an aspect of improving the management or running of the business.
Associated Words: Agenda (noun), Board Meeting (noun), Company Meeting (noun), Motion (noun), To Run a Business (collocation).

Show of Hands (collocation): A show of hands is a way of voting. In company and board meetings a vote can be held by the number of shares or by the number of people who are in attendance at the meeting. If the vote is by the number of people at the meeting then this vote is done by a show of hands.
Associated Words: Board Meeting (noun), Company Meeting (noun).

Special Resolution (noun): This is a type of resolution that requires a higher percentage of approval from the attendees of the meeting. A special resolution is usually a proposal or motion that is more important to the business than an ordinary resolution. As the issues that require a special resolution are more important, over 75% of the attendees at the meeting must vote in favour of it.
Associated Words: Motion (noun), Ordinary Resolution (noun).

To Take Minutes (collocation): To take minutes is a common phrase in business English that means to note down the resolutions, important decisions and comments in a board or company meeting. A person will be delegated to take the minutes of the meeting and they are expected to distribute them to all interested parties afterwards. The minutes are intended to be an accurate record of what is said and voted on.
Associated Words: Took Minutes (past simple), Taken Minutes (3rd form), Board Meeting (noun), Company Meeting (noun), Resolution (noun).

Unanimous (adjective): This means that a motion or proposal in a board or company meeting has been voted on and every voter agrees (to either pass or not pass a resolution).

Associated Words: Unanimously (adverb), Board Meeting (noun), Company Meeting (noun), Motion (noun), To Pass a Resolution (collocation).

6 TERMINATING A BUSINESS

Administration (noun): A company is in administration once an administrator is appointed. An administrator can be appointed by the directors of the company, a secured creditor or by the court. The administrator takes control of the company and tries to continue running the business as a going concern. If this is not possible then the administrator will realise the company's assets for the best possible price to pay off creditors.
Associated Words: Administrator (person), Asset (noun), Company (noun), Creditor (noun), Going Concern (noun), To Realise Assets (collocation).

To Be In (liquidation/administration/receivership) (phrasal verb): This phrasal verb explains the situation of a company or organisation 'being in liquidation, administration or receivership. For instance, it is common to read reports in newspapers or other media where companies 'went into administration' after failing to pay all of their creditors.
Associated Words: Went Into (past simple), Gone Into (3rd form), Creditor (noun) Administration (noun), Liquidation (noun), Receivership (noun).

To Be Placed Into (liquidation/administration/receivership) (phrasal verb): This is the official procedure when the court puts the company or organisation into liquidation, administration or receivership. For example, 'After careful consideration of the all the issues, the court ruled that the company would be placed into receivership'.
Associated Words: Was Placed Into (past simple), Been Placed Into (3rd form), Administration (noun), Liquidation (noun), Receivership (noun).

To Cease Trading (collocation): This means that a company stops running their business activities and does not buy or sell their goods or services as a going concern.
Associated Words: Ceased Trading (past simple), Ceased Trading (3rd form), Going Concern (noun), To Run a Business (collocation).

To Close Down (phrasal verb): This is an informal phrasal verb that means that a company, firm or organisation stops trading and terminates all business activity.

Associated Words: Closed Down (past simple), Closed Down (3rd form), Company (noun).

Compulsory Liquidation (noun): This is a formal court process started by a creditor of the company. The creditor presents a winding up petition to the court stating that the company is unable to pay its debts. The court will consider the facts and may make an order to wind up the company. If the court rules in this way, the Official Receiver becomes the liquidator of the company. Once the liquidation is complete, the company is closed.

Associated Words: Liquidator (person), Company (noun), Creditor (noun), Debt (noun), Official Receiver (person), To Wind Up (phrasal verb).

To Dissolve (verb): This verb is commonly used in relation to the termination of partnerships. If a partnership ends, then it is commonly referred to as dissolved.

Associated Words: Dissolved (past simple), Dissolved (3rd form), Partnership (noun).

To Go Bankrupt (collocation): This is a common collocation that means that a company, firm or organisation is officially made bankrupt.

Associated Words: Went Bankrupt (past simple), Gone Bankrupt (3rd form), Company (noun).

To Go Into (liquidation/administration/receivership) (phrasal verb): This phrasal verb describes the process of entering liquidation, administration or receivership. For example, 'XYZ Ltd has not been able to pay their creditors and so have gone into administration'.

Associated Words: Went Into (past simple), Gone Into (3rd form), Administration (noun), Creditor (noun), Liquidation (noun), Receivership (noun).

Insolvent (adjective): This means that a company, firm or organisation that cannot pay all of its debts. It is important to note that insolvency is not the same as bankruptcy. Bankruptcy is a formal court procedure for insolvent companies.

Associated Words: Insolvency (noun), Solvent (adjective), Bankruptcy (noun), Company (noun).

Voluntary Liquidation (noun): This process starts when the company itself passes a resolution to enter into liquidation because it cannot pay its debts. A liquidator is then appointed. The liquidator will try to realise the assets of the company to pay off the creditors. Once this process is complete, the company is wound up and taken off the register of companies.
Associated Words: Liquidator (person), Asset (noun), Company (noun), Creditor (noun), Debt (noun), To Realise Assets (collocation), To Wind Up (Phrasal verb).

To Realise Assets (collocation): This collocation means to sell or make a profit from the possessions of a company or organisation. The phrase is commonly used when an insolvent company wishes to raise money to pay creditors' debts.
Associated Words: Realised Assets (past simple), Realised Assets (3rd form), Asset (noun), Company (noun), Creditor (noun), Debt (noun), Insolvent (adjective), Profit (noun).

Receivership (noun): This is the process of a company being unable to pay a secured creditor's debt and that creditor appointing a receiver. A secured creditor is a creditor who has a charge over an asset of the company. The creditor can use the secured charge to appoint the receiver. A receiver is an insolvency practitioner who sells the assets of a company that are the subject of secured charges to pay the secured creditors.
Associated Words: Receiver (person), Asset (noun), Company (noun), Creditor (noun), Debt (noun), Secured Charge (noun).

To Run Up Debt (phrasal verb): To run up debt means to get into debt or accumulate debt. It is a more informal phrase in legal English but commonly used to describe a company or individual increasing the level of their debt.
Associated Words: Ran Up (past simple), Run Up (3rd form), Company (noun), Debt (noun).

Solvent (adjective): This adjective is the opposite of insolvent. A solvent company is a company that is in a financial position to be able to pay their debts.

Associated Words: Insolvent (adjective), Company (noun), Debt (noun).

To Strike Off (phrasal verb): This is a legal English phrase that means that a company has been removed from the register of companies, usually because of irregularity or closure.

Associated Words: Struck Off (past simple), Struck Off (3rd form), Company (noun).

To Wind Up (phrasal verb): This phrasal verb is an informal legal English phrase that means that a company or organisation has ceased trading and has entered some form of insolvency proceedings.

Associated Words: Wound Up (past simple), Wound Up (3rd form), To Cease Trading (collocation), Company (noun), Insolvency Proceedings (noun).

7 GLOSSARY

Business Structures

Charity
Consortium
Corporation
Enterprise
Joint Venture
Legal Entity
Limited Liability Partnership
Non-Governmental Organisation
Off-The-Shelf Company
Partnership
Private Limited Company
Public Limited Company
Self-Employed

Setting Up a Business

Articles of Association
To Acquire
Certificate of Incorporation
To Contribute To
To Draw Up
To Go Into Business With
To Incorporate
To Invest In
To Issue Shares
Issued Share Capital
To List
Memorandum of Association
To Merge With
Nominal Value
Partnership Agreement

To Raise Finance
To Register
Registered Office
To Set Up
Share Capital
Shares/Stocks
Stock Exchange
Takeover
To Trade
To Trade Under

People in Business

Accountant
Administrator
Auditor
Board
Chairperson
Company Secretary
Creditor
Debtor
Director
Dormant Partner
Employee
Employer
Equity Partner
Executive Director
Founder
Insolvency Practitioner
Liquidator
Member
Non-Executive Director
Official Receiver
Partner
Proxy
To Resign

To Retire
Salaried Partner
Service Agreement
Shadow Director
Shareholder
Sleeping Partner
Stockbroker

Running a Business

Accounts
Annual Return
Assets
Authorised Share Capital
Balance Sheet
To Close a Deal
Conflict of Interest
Corporation Tax
To Declare a Dividend
To Disclose Information
To Draw
Expenses
Fiduciary Duty
To Fluctuate
To Hold/Own Shares
Income Tax
To Invest
Invoice
Joint and Several Liability
To Lay Off
Liable
Limited Liability
To Make a Loss
To Make Redundant
To Manage
Market Value

Notice
Profit
Profit and Loss Account
Regulations
Return on Investment
To Run a Business
To Subscribe to Shares

Business Meetings

To Adjourn
Agenda
Annual General Meeting
To Appoint
Board Meeting
To Carry a Motion
To Chair a Meeting
Company Meeting
To Convene
To Declare
To Draw Attention To
To Elect
To Exercise (a right or power)
To Expel
Extraordinary General Meeting
Majority
Minority
Minutes
Motion
To Obtain a Majority
Ordinary Resolution
To Pass a Resolution
Poll
To Propose
Quorum
Resolution

Show of Hands
Special Resolution
To Take a Minutes
Unanimous

Terminating a Business

Administration
To Be In (liquidation/administration/receivership)
To Be Placed Into (liquidation/administration/receivership)
To Cease Trading
To Close Down
Compulsory Liquidation
To Dissolve
To Go Bankrupt
To Go Into (liquidation/administration/receivership)
Insolvent
Voluntary Liquidation
To Realise Assets
Receivership
To Run Up Debt
Solvent
To Strike Off
To Wind Up

BUSINESS AND COMPANY LAW

8. EXERCISES

TRUE OR FALSE

Decide if these sentences are true or false (answers are at the back of the book):

1. A general legal English term for a business, organisation or firm is 'Enterprise'.

2. A public limited company is a business structure where two or more partners own the business. The partners are individually liable for any debts of the business.

3. A person who works for themselves and does not need to incorporate a company or register as an employee is called 'self-employed'. They are individually liable for their business debts.

4. The nominal value of a share is its original share value. Commonly, a company newly incorporated with the company registrar will have a nominal value or £1 per share.

5. The registered office is the official business address of the company. The address is used to receive all official business correspondence.

6. The legal English term that describes the situation when a company takes control or acquires another company, usually by purchasing a majority shareholding, is called a liquidation.

7. The board of the company is a group of employees and shareholders who make important decisions in relation to running the business.

8. A director of a company is a person who has a formal decision-making position in the company. They owe a fiduciary duty to act in the best interests of the company.

9. The name of the company or organisation that employs a person is called the employer. The name of the person who works for the employer is the employee.

10. The legal English verb used to describe the situation when a person reaches the age of retirement, stops working and receives a pension is 'to resign'.

11. An asset is a possession that has a value. This can be a physical object such as a building, or something intangible, for instance a good reputation.

12. The cost incurred by employees and directors of a company is called a dividend. Examples include travel expenses and accommodation costs when travelling on business.

13. The legal English verb used to describe the action of buying shares, equipment or anything else to improve and move the business forward is 'to invest'.

14. Giving notice means to notify another party that something has been done or is going to be done. The term is usually used in relation to contracts, especially the termination of contracts.

15. The formal plan of topics to be discussed at a company or a board meeting is called the motion. It is usually circulated to the attendees of the meeting in advance.

16. A company meeting is only attended by the directors of a company.

17. A report of what is said, voted on and passed as resolutions at company and board meetings is called an agenda. It is usually circulated to all the attendees after the meeting. It can be used as an official record of decision making in a company.

18. An ordinary resolution requires 50% plus one vote to be passed at a company or board meeting.

19. A unanimous vote means that over 75% of the attendees vote in favour of a motion.

20. Compulsory liquidation is the process where a creditor of a company presents a winding up petition to the court stating that the debtor company is unable to pay its debts.

VOCABULARY GAP FILL

Complete the sentences with the missing word or phrase (answers are at the back of the book):

1. The common name for a business structure that is a non-profit making organisation run for the benefit of others is a _____.

2. A _____ venture is a business agreement or enterprise where two or more parties co-operate for a specific project, usually for a limited period of time.

3. An _____-_____-_____ company is an existing company that has been incorporated but is not actually in use. Off-the-shelf companies are available for individuals or other companies to start trading quickly, without needing to go through the incorporation process.

4. In business and company law, partners _____ capital to the partnership in order to receive a percentage of the profits. This means they give or provide money for the partnership.

5. A company's _____ _____ _____ is a formal document that states the basic information of the company. It is one of the most important documents, together with the articles of association and the certificate of incorporation.

6. If a company wishes to trade their shares on a _____ _____ then it must apply to be 'listed'. The procedure of applying to be listed is also known as 'floatation'. Once listed, the shares are made public for trading.

7. XYZ ltd needs a loan to pay for new equipment. They go to a bank who agrees to lend the company money. In this situation, the bank is the _____ and XYZ ltd is the debtor.

8. A _____ partner is not involved in the day to day running of the partnership but will receive a proportional share of any profits. They usually provide financial investment to the partnership.

9. All formal insolvency proceedings should be carried out by a licensed

172

_____ _____. They have authority to conduct insolvency proceedings such as administration and bankruptcy proceedings.

10. The _____ _____ _____ examines a company's financial records, makes background enquiries and reports back to creditors and shareholders of the company. Their main role is to sell the assets of the company and distribute the proceeds to the creditors. Their duty is to the court in insolvency proceedings.

11. A _____ director offers the executive and non-executive directors advice and expertise on specific issues. They are not usually an official director of a company.

12. A _____ is a person who buys and sells stocks and shares on the stock market or stock exchange. They act as an agent for their clients and will charge a fee or commission for the transactions.

13. A 'snapshot' of a company's finances at any given point in time is called a _____ sheet.

14. The legal English verb that describes an equity partner receiving their remuneration as an agreed amount every month is called to _____.

15. _____ _____ duty means a director must act in the best interests of the company, to act in good faith at all times and declare any conflicts of interest.

16. *'We do not have quorum for the meeting today. We have no choice but to _____ the meeting until next Tuesday'*.

17. The verb used in business and company law to describe the act of organising a company or board meeting is to _____.

18. A _____ is a formal legal English term that means proposal. The attendees of the meeting will vote on these proposals and, if successful, it will pass as a resolution.

19. A common informal verb used in business and company law to describe terminating a business is to _____.

20. The process of a company being unable to pay a secured creditor's debt and that creditor appointing a receiver is called _____.

PREPOSITION GAP FILL

Complete the sentences using the correct preposition (answers are at the back of the book):

1. The articles _____ association (also known simply as 'articles') set out the responsibilities, rules and regulations of the management of the company. These articles will define what the company can do, the roles and duties of the directors and the extent of the powers of the shareholders.

2. The official document that states a company is legally established and all relevant documentation has been filed with the authorities is called the Certificate _____ Incorporation.

3. When a partnership is created it is common for the parties to 'draw _____' a partnership agreement to set out the important details.

4. To go _____ business with someone means to co-operate or collaborate.

5. The phrasal verb used when an individual or organisation puts money into a business is to invest _____ a business.

6. *'Last year, the US firm Blackthorne & co merged _____ a German law firm based in Berlin. This means that they now form one business entity.'*

7. To set _____ a company means to establish or form a company. It is an informal phrase but commonly used in legal and business English.

8. A common example of a conflict _____ interest is when a director of a company also holds a personal interest that conflicts with the best interests of the company.

9. *'After careful consideration of the all the issues, the court ruled that the company would be placed _____ receivership.'*

10. *'Unfortunately, the company has had to make the difficult decision to lay _____* *a number of the marketing team. This is due to a re-structuring and cost reduction exercise.'*

11. Another way to say to buy shares in a private or public company is to subscribe _____ shares.

12. *'Welcome to the board meeting. I would like to start by drawing your attention _____ item number 1 on the agenda, this is to discuss the new company logo.'*

13. If a company or board meeting vote is by the number of people at the meeting, then this vote is called a show _____ hands.

14. *The company could not pay all their debtors and subsequently went _____ administration in the following year.'*

15. The profit made on the sale of an asset is also known as a return _____ the investment. For example, if a real estate business acquires a property in order to renovate and improve its condition, it may then sell the property at a higher price they bought it for.

16. *'ABC Ltd have not been able to pay their creditors and so have gone _____ administration.'*

17. An informal phrase in legal English commonly used to describe a company or individual increasing the level of their debt is to run _____ debt.

18. To strike _____ means that a company has been officially removed from the companies registrar. This is usually because the company has requested to be removed or it has been removed due to irregularity.

19. One of most common informal phrasal verbs that means that a company has ceased trading and has entered some type of insolvency proceeding is called to wind _____ a company.

20. To close _____ is an informal business and company law phrase that means a company stops trading and terminates all business activity.

COLLOCATION GAP FILL

Complete the sentences using the correct collocation (answers are at the back of the book):

1. To _____ shares means to distribute or transfer shares in a company to an investor or shareholder.

2. The collocation that means to find or produce an amount of money or capital is to _____ finance.

3. Many companies use a different trading name to their official registered company name. For instance, a company registered 'International Operations Global Inc' may choose to trade _____ a shorter and simpler name.

4. When a company officially announces whether or not a dividend is to be paid to its shareholders, the legal English term used is to _____ a dividend.

5. To _____ information means to send or show information to a relevant person on a formal basis.

6. _____ and _____ liability means that if there is a group of two or more people liable for a judgment debt then all of the members of the group are liable individually and also together as a group.

7. If a party is legally responsible for their actions or omissions the legal English term is that they are _____ for their acts or omissions.

8. To _____ a loss means that a company or other organisation has spent more money than they have received.

9. When a company decides to re-structure the work force and reduce the number of their employees, these employees are _____ redundant.

10. A financial document that shows the income and expenses of a business for a financial year is called a _____ and _____ account.

11. The legal English phrase to _____ a business means to organise and manage a business on a day-to-day basis.

12. If a motion or proposal in a company or board meeting is passed and approved by way of a vote, a common phrase used is to _____ a motion.

13. The person who _____ a meeting is called a chairperson and usually will hold the casting vote in the event of a tie between the other attendees.

14. To _____ a right or power means to use that right or power in a company or board meeting. For instance, shareholders or directors can use their right to vote, their right to abstain from voting or use their right to vote by proxy.

15. To _____ a majority means to get or receive a majority. In a legal English context, it is used when there are enough 'Yes' votes for a motion to pass and become a resolution in a board or company meeting.

16. When a motion or proposal receives enough votes for it to be approved, the legal English phrase is that the motion or proposal is _____ as a resolution.

17. A company or board meeting will usually have a designated person to _____ minutes of the meeting. This to note down the resolutions, important decisions and comments in a board or company meeting.

18. To _____ trading means that a company stops running their business activities and does not buy or sell their goods or services as a going concern.

19. To _____ bankrupt is a simple way of stating that a company has entered into bankruptcy.

20. To _____ assets means to sell or make a profit from the possessions of a company or organisation.

REPLACE THE INCORRECT WORD

Replace the *incorrect* word with the correct one (answers are at the back of the book):

1. Once a *partnership* [_____] is incorporated it becomes a separate legal entity. This means that it has its own legal personality and can sue and be sued.

2. A *sole trader* [_____   _____] has its own legal personality and can issue proceedings or have proceedings issued against it. Common examples are private limited companies and charities.

3. A *public* [_____] limited company is run by the directors and owned by its shareholders (also known as members or subscribers). Shares can only be bought with the company's express permission.

4. To *certify* [_____] a company is the process of formally establishing a company and successfully registering it with the relevant authorities.

5. The number of shares that the company has issued in total to shareholders at the nominal amount is called the *authorised* [_____] share capital.

6. A new company called Great Scott Ltd is set up. Upon incorporation, it issued 2,000 shares at £1 each. Recently it issued 500 more shares, also at £1 each. The total share *count* [_____] of Great Scott Ltd is now £2,500.

7. A *company secretary* [_____] is a person from an external company, for example, an accountancy firm, who will investigate and examine a company's accounts.

8. A *shareholder* [_____   _____] is responsible for filing all relevant legal documentation with the authorities, for example, annual returns and share registers.

9. A *creditor* [_____] is a person or organisation that owes money to someone. For instance, a company that has a loan with a bank.

10. A person who can vote on a motion in a company or board meeting on behalf of a shareholder or board member who is not able to attend is called a *sleeping partner* [_____] .

11. The document used for a company to update its details every year in relation to directors, shareholders, accounts and other information is called a *divided* [_____   _____] .

12. The maximum amount of share capital that a company is allowed to issue to shareholders is called the *nominal* [_____] share capital.

13. The verb to *invest* [_____] is commonly used with share prices to describe the movement of the price rising or falling.

14. An *extraordinary* [_____] general meeting is a company meeting of shareholders held once a year. Shareholders discuss the most important aspects of company management, including financial results and the directors.

15. The verb to *adjourn* [_____] , in business and legal English, is commonly used to describe the situation of notifying and paying shareholders a dividend.

16. A *minority* [_____] vote is when more than half of the total votes are cast in favour of a proposal or motion.

17. An *agenda* [_____] is the smallest number of people that need to be present at a company or board meeting before it can officially begin and before official decisions can be made.

18. During the process of *incorporation* [_____], an administrator can be appointed by the directors of the company, a secured creditor or by the court. The administrator takes control of the company and tries to continue running the business as a going concern.

19. To be *solvent* [_____] means that a company, firm or organisation cannot pay all of its debts.

20. The process of *takeover* [_____] starts when the company itself passes a resolution to enter into liquidation because it cannot pay its debts. A liquidator is then appointed.

9 ANSWERS

True or False:

1. True

2. False

3. True

4. True

5. True

6. False

7. False

8. True

9. True

10. False

11. True

12. False

13. True

14. True

15. False

16. False

17. False

18. True

19. False

20. True

Vocabulary Gap Fill:

1. charity

2. joint

3. off-the-shelf

4. contribute

5. Memorandum of Association

6. stock exchange

7. creditor

8. dormant

9. insolvency practitioner

10. official receiver

11. shadow

12. stockbroker

13. balance

14. draw

15. Fiduciary

16. adjourn

17. convene

18. motion

19. dissolve

20. receivership

Prepositions Gap Fill:

1. of

2. of

3. up

4. into

5. in

6. with

7. up

8. of

9. into

10. off

11. to

12. to

13. of

14. into

15. on

16. into

17. up

18. off

19. up

20. down

Collocations Gap Fill:

1. issue

2. raise

3. under

4. declare

5. disclose

6. Joint/several

7. liable

8. make

9. made

10. profit/loss

11. run

12. carry

13. chairs

14. exercise

15. obtain

16. passed

17. take

18. cease

19. go

20. realise

Replace the Incorrect Word

1. ~~partnership,~~ corporation

2. ~~sole trader~~, legal entity

3. ~~public~~, private

4. ~~certify~~, incorporate

5. ~~authorised~~, issued

6. ~~count~~, capital

7. ~~company secretary~~, auditor

8. ~~shareholder~~, company secretary

9. ~~creditor~~, debtor

10. ~~sleeping partner~~, proxy

11. ~~dividend~~, annual return

12. ~~nominal~~, authorised

13. ~~invest~~, fluctuate

14. ~~extraordinary~~, annual

15. ~~adjourn~~, declare

16. ~~minority~~, majority

17. ~~agenda~~, quorum

18. ~~incorporation~~, administration

19. ~~solvent~~, insolvent

20. ~~takeover~~, voluntary liquidation

D. DISPUTE RESOLUTION AND LITGATION DICTIONARY

1. BEFORE A CLAIM

Adjudication (noun): This is a type of alternative dispute resolution commonly used in construction and building disputes. If there is a dispute over a building or construction contract, the contract will usually have a clause that requires the parties to attend adjudication proceedings before any litigation can be brought.
Associated Words: To Adjudicate (verb), Alternative Dispute Resolution (noun), Dispute (noun), Litigation (noun).

To Allege (verb): This verb is used in legal English when one person thinks that another person has done something wrong. For example, if Mr Jones thinks that Miss Davis crashed her car into his car, then he alleges that Miss Davis has committed the tort of negligence. Another way to say this is that he is "making an allegation against Miss Davis". It is important to remember that the tort (or crime) has not been proven in a court of law. It is only an opinion of a person's wrong doing or guilt at this stage. In criminal law you will also see the verb "to accuse" which has a similar meaning.
Associated Words: Alleged (past simple), Alleged (3rd form), Allegation (noun), To Make an Allegation Against Someone (collocation), Negligence (noun), Tort (noun).

Alternative Dispute Resolution "ADR" (noun): This is a common alternative to litigation. ADR has become more popular in recent years as it is seen as a faster, cheaper and more effective way to settle disputes without using the courts. Mediation is the most common form of ADR. It is also common for the court to order that the parties attempt to settle the case via ADR if possible before a trial is scheduled.

Associated Words: Case (noun), Dispute (noun), To Order (verb), To Settle (verb), Trial (noun).

Arbitration (noun): This is a process similar to litigation but with less formalities and legal procedure. The main aim of arbitration is to settle the dispute early. It is very common in international contracts and many standard contracts will have an arbitration clause. The clause will usually require all parties to attend arbitration before litigation proceedings are issued. There are specific rules for arbitration proceedings in England and Wales and it is becoming a useful alternative to court proceedings. There are also many conventions and institutions which govern international arbitration and, similarly, these are seen as a useful alternative to formal legal proceedings.
Associated Words: Contract law (noun), Dispute (noun), Litigation (noun), Proceedings (noun), To Settle (verb).

To Breach (verb): This is a very important word in civil litigation and dispute resolution. It means that someone has broken an agreement or has not done something that they should have done. It is commonly used in tort and in contract law, for example "breach of terms and conditions", "breach of obligations" or "breach of duty of care".
Associated Words: Breached (past simple), Breached (3rd form), Breach (noun), Duty of Care (noun), Litigation (noun), Obligations (noun).

Causation (noun): This is the connection between the defendant's breach and the loss suffered by the claimant. For instance, the tort of negligence requires that causation is established for the court to find in favour of the claimant. In other words the claimant must show that the acts or omissions of the defendant caused loss to the claimant.
Associated Words: To Cause (verb), Caused (past simple), Caused (3rd form), Claimant (noun), Defendant (noun), Loss (noun), Negligence (noun), To Omit (verb).

Carelessness (noun): Carelessness is a common English word that is used to describe the legal English term negligence. It means that somebody does not show enough concern or awareness about the possible consequences of their actions.

Associated Words: Careless (adjective), Negligence (noun).

Civil Procedure Rules (noun): These rules are commonly known as the CPR. They are the rules that must be followed in civil litigation cases in England and Wales. The rules were introduced in 1999 by Lord Woolf. The aim of the rules is to provide an easier, quicker and fairer system for all litigants. All lawyers who are involved in dispute resolution should be familiar with these rules in England and Wales.
Associated Words: Litigation (noun), Litigant (noun), Woolf Report (noun).

To Commit (verb): We use this verb when someone does something criminal or that is classed as a tort. For example, if someone steals something, we say that they have committed theft. If someone causes an accident, we say that they have committed negligence. To commit is used in both criminal law and civil law. It is not correct to say "to do/make theft" or "to do/make negligence". The correct verb to use is "to commit".
Associated Words: Committed (past simple), Committed (3rd form), Committed (adjective), Commission (noun), Negligence (noun), Tort (noun).

To Dispute (verb): This verb means to argue about something or to question something. It is used in legal English both as a verb and as a noun. The noun "dispute" is a situation when two or more people disagree about something. Civil litigation claims are also commonly called disputes.
Associated Words: Disputed (past simple), Disputed (3rd form), Dispute (noun), Disputed (adjective), Litigation (noun).

Duty of Care (noun): Under the law of tort an individual owes a duty of care to other individuals not to cause any damage or harm to them. This means that they need to be careful or responsible in certain situations. This concept came from common law and has developed over many years in the English courts. The duty of care is one part of establishing the tort of negligence. To establish whether there is a duty of care, the court will generally look at three things. First, was harm reasonably foreseeable. Second, were the claimant and defendant in close proximity, and third is it fair and reasonable to impose a duty of care on the defendant in this situation. If the situation satisfies these three conditions, the court is likely to conclude that a duty of care has arisen.

Associated Words: Claimant (noun), Common Law (noun), Defendant (noun), Foreseeable (noun), Negligence (noun), (noun), Tort (noun).

Foreseeable (adjective): This means that something is predictable or expected. The concept of whether an act or omission is foreseeable is an important concept of dispute resolution. Foreseeability is especially important in the areas of tort law and breach of contract. The court will look at foreseeability to help establish whether a defendant owes a claimant a duty of care and whether it was foreseeable that a defendant's acts or omissions caused loss or harm.

Associated Words: To Foresee (verb), Foresaw (past simple), Foreseen (3rd form), Foreseeability (noun), Breach of Contract (noun), Claimant (noun), Defendant (noun), Tort Law (noun).

Governing Law (noun): This is more informally known as the choice of law or applicable law. It is a very common issue in contract law. In legal English governing law means the country, state or jurisdiction where legal proceedings will be heard if the parties have a dispute. It is common for both parties to agree the governing law before executing a contract, however, it is also common for governing law to become a contentious matter if there is no clause in the contract or if the clause is not clear.

Associated Words: Applicable Law (noun), Contentious (adjective), Contract Law (noun), Dispute (noun), Jurisdiction (noun), Matter (noun), Party (noun).

Grounds (noun): This is the legal English word for the reason or the basis of a claim. For instance, you may often hear "what are the grounds for this claim?". This means, what are the reasons for the claim, or what happened to cause the claim. For example, Mr Smith sued the local supermarket for negligence on the grounds that they failed to clear water from the shop floor. Mr Smith slipped on the water and broke his arm. This means that the reason Mr Smith sued the supermarket was because they had failed to clear the water.

Associated Words: Claim (noun), To Sue (verb).

To Harm (verb): This verb means to damage or to hurt somebody or something. In civil litigation and dispute resolution it is important to establish or prove that the claimant has been harmed or has suffered loss.
Associated Words: Harmed (past simple), Harmed (3rd form), Harm (noun), Claimant (noun), Litigation (noun), Loss (noun), To Suffer (verb).

To Infringe (verb): This means the same as the verb "to breach", however it is only used in certain collocations and contexts. To infringe is usually used with human rights and intellectual property law. Common collocations in human rights law are to infringe freedom of speech, freedom of movement or freedom of religion. Common collocations in intellectual property law are to infringe copyright, trademarks or patents.
Associated Words: Infringed (past simple), Infringed (3rd form), Infringed (adjective), Infringement (noun), To Breach (verb), Copyright (noun), Human Rights (noun), Patent (noun), Trademark (noun).

Injured Party (noun): An injured party is an individual or organisation who has suffered harm or loss. In legal English the injured party is usually the claimant but it can also be the defendant, for instance in a counterclaim.
Associated Words: Claimant (noun), Counterclaim (noun), Defendant (noun), Harm (noun), Litigation (noun), Loss (noun).

Letter Before Action (noun): This is a letter sent from the claimant to the defendant before a claim is issued. The aim of this letter is to inform the defendant of the possibility of a claim and the details of the claimant's arguments. Due to the Civil Procedure Rules, it is usual practice for a letter before action to be sent before a claim is issued.
Associated Words: Civil Procedure Rules (noun), Claim (noun), Claimant (noun), Defendant (noun), To Issue (verb).

Litigation (noun): This means the process of contesting a dispute in the law courts. It is commonly used in civil law to describe the situation and procedure of a claim being issued by the claimant against the defendant.
Associated Words: Claimant (noun), Defendant (noun), Dispute (noun), To Issue (verb).

Loss (noun): Loss means that something or someone has suffered damage or harm. In order to bring an action in civil litigation the claimant must have suffered loss. Loss can be financial, physical or mental harm.
Associated Words: Claimant (noun), Harm (noun), Litigation (noun), To Suffer (verb).

To Omit (verb): This verb means that someone failed to do something that they should have done. In legal English, to omit is commonly used in relation to the tort of negligence, especially when considering a breach of a duty of care. A breach can be a negligent act or a negligent omission. A negligent omission is when a person does not do something and this causes another person to suffer harm. For example, if a building company fails to keep their building site safe, this is a negligent omission which may result in harm to an individual if they have an accident and hurt themselves. A negligent omission to act can lead to a claim in the civil courts.
Associated Words: Omitted (past simple), Omitted (3rd form), Omission (noun), To Breach (verb), To Cause (verb), Claim (noun), Duty of Care (noun), Harm (noun), Negligence (noun), To Suffer (verb), Tort (noun).

Overriding Objective (noun): The overriding objective is a principle from the Civil Procedure Rules. The purpose of the overriding objective is for the civil litigation and dispute resolution process to be fair, fast and inexpensive. The principle is that each case should be treated proportionally in relation to the size, importance and complexity of the claim and the financial situation of both parties. The court must consider the overriding objective when they make rulings, give directions and interpret the Civil Procedure Rules.
Associated Words: Civil Procedure Rules (noun), Litigation (noun).

Practice Direction (noun): These are the rules that support the Civil Procedure Rules. Each rule in the Civil Procedure Rules has a Practice Direction that provides further information on the rules.
Associated Words: Civil Procedure Rules (noun).

Pre-Action Protocol (noun): Some types of claims, for example personal injury and defamation claims, must follow a specific pre-action protocol. This means that they have to follow special rules in the Civil Procedure Rules before issuing a claim. The pre-action protocols are designed to encourage openness and an early exchange of information to assist a negotiated settlement before the need for litigation. Under the pre-action protocols both parties must exchange information in relation to the dispute, open discussions for settlement and try to avoid bringing proceedings.

Associated Words: Civil Procedure Rules (noun), Defamation (noun), Dispute (noun), Litigation (noun), To Negotiate (verb), Personal Injury (noun), To Settle (verb).

To Resolve (verb): This word is similar in meaning to settle but it is usually used in the collocations "to resolve a dispute" or "to resolve a conflict". It means that an argument or disagreement is settled or agreed to end. Due to the nature of the Civil Procedure Rules the term "Dispute Resolution" has now become attached to Civil Litigation. Some law firms now refer to their litigation departments as dispute resolution departments.

Associated Words: Resolved (past simple), Resolved (3rd form), Resolution (noun), Conflict (noun), To Settle (verb).

To Settle (verb): This word means to resolve a dispute with the agreement of all the parties. It is a very important word in legal English as the concept of civil litigation changed with the Civil Procedure Rules. The emphasis of the Civil Procedure Rules is on settling claims and avoiding proceedings if possible. The collocation "to settle a claim" is very common in legal English.

Associated Words: Settled (past simple), Settled (3rd form), Settled (adjective), Settlement (noun), Claim (noun), Civil Procedure Rules (noun), Dispute (noun), Litigation (noun), Proceedings (noun), To Resolve (verb).

To Suffer (verb): This verb means to experience something negative. In legal English it is commonly used with harm, loss and damage. The phrases "to suffer harm", "to suffer loss" and "to suffer damage" are all collocations used in litigation to describe the claimant experiencing something negative because of the defendant's acts or omissions.

Associated Words: Suffered (past simple), Suffered (3rd form), Suffered (adjective), Suffering (noun), Claimant (noun), Defendant (noun), Harm (noun), Loss (noun), To Omit (verb).

Woolf Report (noun): This report produced the Civil Procedure Rules. The report, formally known as "The Access to Justice Report", was written in 1996 to help the individual's right to justice. In his report, Lord Woolf, a former barrister, recommended a number of ideas to help individuals achieve justice. For instance, the report says that the legal system should be fair, fast, inexpensive, understandable, effective and well organised.

Associated Words: Barrister (noun), Civil Procedure Rules (noun).

2 MAKING A CLAIM

Affidavit (noun): This Latin word means to declare an oath made in writing. An oath means a formal promise. The collocation to "swear an affidavit" is commonly used in legal English, however the recent movement away from legalese has caused the phrase to be replaced in the Civil Procedure Rules with "Statement of Truth". The word affidavit is still used in certain situations and in the US legal system.
Associated Words: Civil Procedure Rules (noun), Statement of Truth (noun).

Barrister (person): This is a type of lawyer in England and Wales. In the English legal system there are two types of lawyer. One type is called a solicitor and the other is called a barrister. A barrister will usually do the advocacy in a case after receiving instructions from the solicitor. Barristers are specifically trained in the skill of advocacy and legal procedure. They are famous for their court dress of long black gown and horse-hair wig and are also known as "members of the Bar".
Associated Words: Advocacy (noun), Solicitor (person).

To Brief (verb): This verb means to instruct. It is used in legal English when the client instructs or "briefs" a lawyer. To brief a lawyer means to give them information or instructions in relation to the case or claim. The word "brief" as a noun is sometimes used to describe a lawyer.
Associated Words: Briefed (past simple), Briefed (3ʳᵈ form), Briefing (noun), Case (noun), Claim (noun), To Instruct (verb).

To Bring an Action (collocation): This means to issue proceedings. It is a common, formal phrase in legal English and can be used in a number of collocations, for example to bring a case or to bring a claim. It is also important to note that in legal English a claim is brought "against" someone. The full collocation would be "to bring an action against" (the defendant).
Associated Words: Brought an Action Against (past simple), Brought an Action Against (3ʳᵈ form), Case (noun), Claim (noun), To Issue (verb).

Burden of Proof (noun): This means that one party has the obligation of proving their case in court. The burden of proof in civil litigation "rests" with the claimant. This means that the claimant must prove their case on the balance of probabilities. This means that they must show the court that their version of the facts is more likely than the defendant's version. The burden of proof in criminal law is defined differently and rests with the prosecution to prove their case so that the jury or judge is sure of the defendant's guilt.
Associated Words: Balance of Probabilities (noun), Claimant (noun), Defendant (noun), Obligation (noun).

Case (noun): This word is a general term that means matter or claim.
Associated Words: Claim (noun), Matter (noun).

To Claim (verb): In legal English this verb means to declare that somebody has harmed or injured you so that you deserve compensation for your loss. For example, Mr Smith claimed that Dr Roberts was negligent when he incorrectly diagnosed Mr Smith's medical condition and that this caused Mr Smith physical injury. The noun "claim" is also commonly used to describe a case or legal proceedings. The collocations "to make a claim" or "to bring a claim" are common in civil litigation.
Associated Words: Claimed (past simple), Claimed (3rd form), Claim (noun), Case (noun), To Harm, (verb).

Claimant (noun): This is the name of the party who issues a claim or proceedings.
Associated Words: Claim (noun), To Issue (verb).

Claim Form (noun): This is the name of a document used to issue a claim. The claim form contains the basic information on the parties, the grounds for the claim and the remedy. If the facts and grounds of the claim are complicated, the claimant can also file a longer version of the claim form called the particulars of claim.
Associated Words: Claim (noun), Claimant (noun), To Issue (verb), Grounds (noun), Particulars of Claim (noun), Parties (noun).

Court Fee (noun): This is an amount of money that the claimant must pay to the court when they issue the claim. The fee pays for the administration costs of the case.
Associated Words: Case (noun), Claim (noun), Claimant (noun), To Issue (verb).

Evidence (noun): This word means all the data and information used by the parties when they try to prove their case in court. Evidence can be produced in different ways, for example, it can be a written or oral witness statement, documents, objects, videos, phone records etc. Please note that evidence is an uncountable noun ("evidences" is not a word in English). To use evidence as a countable noun, the word "exhibits" can be used, especially for physical types of evidence.
Associated Words: Exhibit (noun), Witness Statement (noun).

Exhibit (noun): As stated above this word can be used in the same way as evidence but as a countable noun. It is usually used for physical types of evidence as stated above.
Associated Word: Evidence (noun).

To File (verb): This means to send or place with the court. Some common legal English collocations are "to file a claim" and "to file an application".
Associated Words: Filed (past simple), Filed (3rd form), To File a Claim (collocation), To File an Application (collocation).

To Issue (verb): The collocations "to issue a claim" and "to issue proceedings" are the formal legal English phrases that mean to start a claim or case in court. A claim is issued on the date the claim form is received by the court. The court will stamp the claim form to indicate that it has received all the correct documentation and the correct fee has been paid. After the court fee has been paid and the court has stamped the claim form, the claim has officially been issued.
Associated Words: Issued (past simple), Issued (3rd form), Issued (adjective), Claim Form (noun), To Issue a Claim (collocation), Fee (noun), To Issue Proceedings (collocation).

Issue (noun): This noun means a point or question that is in dispute.
Associated Word: Dispute (noun).

Limitation (noun): After the date of the defendant's breach (or the date that the breach was discovered), the claimant has a limited period of time to issue the claim form at the court. This is called the limitation period. If the claimant tries to issue a claim after the limitation period, the court may decide that the claim is "time-barred". If a claim is time-barred then the court will not hear the claim.
Associated Words: To Breach (verb), Claim (noun), Claimant (noun), Defendant (noun), To Hear (verb).

Litigant in Person (noun): This is an individual or organisation who represents themselves in court. They are not represented by a barrister or a solicitor.
Associated Words: Barrister (person), To Represent (verb), Solicitor (person).

Particulars of Claim (noun): This document is a longer version of the claim form that the claimant issues at court. The particulars of claim are for claims that are more complicated or need a more detailed explanation.
Associated Words: Claim (noun), Claimant (noun), Claim Form (noun), To Issue at Court (collocation).

Plaintiff (noun): This is the old legal English word for claimant. The Civil Procedure Rules changed this term. Plaintiff is still used in the US legal system.
Associated Words: Civil Procedure Rules (noun), Claimant (noun).

To Plead (verb): This verb means to declare or state your case or position to the court. The noun "pleading" is an old legal English word that means statement of case.
Associated Words: Pleaded (past simple), Pleaded (3rd form), Pleading (noun), Case (noun).

Proceedings (noun): This word has two main meanings in legal English. The first meaning is the ongoing process of a claim. For instance, "The proceedings have been unusually slow in this case". The second meaning of the word proceedings is the claim itself. For example, "Mr Pitt brought proceedings against Mrs Jones for breach of contract".
Associated Words: To Bring Proceedings (collocation), Breach of Contract (noun), Claim (noun).

To Serve (verb): This verb means to send or give documents to another party in the claim. It is a very important concept in civil litigation because there are very strict rules on how and in what time period documents must be served on the defendant(s). For example, after the claimant issues the claim with the court, the claimant must then serve the claim form on the defendant. The defendant must then serve the defence on the claimant. The correct collocation to use in legal English is "to serve (the document) on someone".
Associated Words: Served (past simple), Served (3rd form), Service (noun), To Serve (documents) on someone (collocation), Claim (noun), Claimant (noun), Claim Form (noun), Defendant (noun), To Issue (verb).

Solicitor (person): A solicitor is a qualified legal advisor who has finished their law studies and practical training to become a lawyer in England and Wales. However, in England and Wales there are two types of lawyer (see barrister above). A solicitor gives legal advice, researches legal points, drafts letters and contracts and represents clients in court. The main difference between a barrister and a solicitor is that a solicitor needs a higher "right of audience" to represent clients in the higher courts, for example, the Court of Appeal. A right of audience is permission to represent and speak for your client in court. Barristers automatically have higher rights of audience.
Associated Words: Advocacy (noun), Barrister (person), Court (noun), Court of Appeal (noun).

Statement of Case (noun): This is a formal document used in civil litigation in which a party can state their arguments or positions. For example, the particulars of claim, the defence and the reply to defence are all statements of case. There are rules in the Civil Procedure Rules that provide for the form and the time limits when all statements of case must be filed with the court and served on other parties.

Associated Words: Case (noun), Claim (noun), Civil Procedure Rules (noun), To File a Document (collocation), To Serve a Document (collocation).

Statement of Truth (noun): This is a phrase that follows certain documents stating that the contents of the documents are true. In civil litigation all statements of case, witness statements, acknowledgements of service and many other types of documents have a statement of truth. For example, a witness statement must include the phrase "I believe that the facts as stated in the witness statement are true". The witness must then sign the statement of truth.

Associated Words: Acknowledgement of Service (noun), Case (noun), Witness Statement (noun).

To Submit (verb): This means to suggest or propose. It is used in legal English when an advocate suggests or states an opinion to the court. For example, "I submit to the court that Mrs Jones breached her duty of care to the claimant". At the end of the trial both advocates give "submissions" to the court. This is similar to a summary of the evidence of their case.

Associated Words: Submitted (past simple), Submitted (3rd form), Submission (noun), To Breach (verb), Case (noun), Claimant (noun), Duty of Care (noun), Loss (noun), Trial (noun).

Third Party (noun): This is a party who may not be a part of the proceedings, but they do have an interest or receive a type of benefit or detriment in relation to the claim.

Associated Words: Claim (noun), Party (noun), Proceedings (noun).

3 DEFENDING A CLAIM

Acknowledgement of Service (noun): This is a document that the defendant must complete and file at court. The document asks the defendant if they admit, deny or acknowledge the claim. To acknowledge means that you know something has happened or that it exists.
Associated Words: To Acknowledge (verb), To Admit (verb), Defendant (noun), To Deny (verb).

To Admit (verb): To admit something means that you confess that you did it or that you are liable for something you did.
Associated Words: Admitted (past simple), Admitted (3rd Form), Admission (noun), Liable (adjective).

Contributory Negligence (noun): This means that the defendant alleges that the claimant caused some of the harm or loss suffered in the claim. If the court agrees, then the amount of damages awarded to the claimant may be reduced. This is because the court believes that the claimant contributed to their own loss.
Associated Words: To Allege (verb), To Cause (verb), Claim (noun), Claimant (noun), Harm (noun), Loss (noun).

To Counterclaim (verb): A counterclaim is a claim made by the defendant against the claimant regarding the same or related issues as the claimant's original claim.
Associated Words: Counterclaimed (past simple), Counterclaimed (3rd form), Counterclaim (noun), Claimant (noun), Defendant (noun).

Default Judgment (noun): This is a ruling by the court that means that one party wins the case because of a failure to act or a lack of response from the other party. It is common for a claimant to be granted default judgment (also known as judgment in default) when a defendant does not respond to a claim.
Associated Words: Claim (noun), Claimant (noun), Defendant (noun), To Be Granted Judgment in Default (collocation).

To Defend (verb): This verb means that you deny all or some of the allegations stated in the claim form and particulars of claim. The statement of case for a defendant is called a defence and must be filed at court and served on the other parties. The defence will explain the defendant's version of the events that are stated by the claimant in the particulars of claim and the claim form.

Associated Words: Defended (past simple), Defended (3rd form), Defence (noun), Defendant (noun), Allegation (noun), Claim (noun), Claimant (noun), To Deny (verb), To File at Court (collocation), Particulars of Claim (noun), To Serve on a Party (collocation), Statement of Case (noun).

To Deny (verb): To deny something means to state that you did not do something or that you are not liable for something. It is opposite to the verb to admit. The collocation "to deny allegations" is very common in civil litigation and dispute resolution.

Associated Words: Denied (past simple), Denied (3rd form), Denial (noun), Denied (adjective), Denial (noun), To Admit (verb), Allegations (noun), Liable (adjective).

Mitigation of Loss (collocation): This is a concept in common law that means that a person who has suffered loss must take reasonable action to stop or reduce any further loss or damage. If the defendant can establish in court that the claimant did not mitigate their loss, the court may reduce the award for damages to the claimant.

Associated Words: To Mitigate (verb), To Award (verb), Claimant (noun), Common Law (noun), Damages (noun), Loss (noun), To Suffer (verb).

To Respond (verb): The verb to respond means to answer or reply. For instance, under the provisions of the Civil Procedure Rules, once a defendant receives a claim form they have a set period of time in which to respond.

Associated Words: Responded (past simple), Responded (3rd form), Response (noun), Claim Form, (noun), Civil Procedure Rules (noun).

4 COURT PROCEEDINGS

Admissible (adjective): Admissible evidence is evidence that is allowed or admitted to court. Most evidence is admissible, but an example of inadmissible evidence is hearsay evidence. Hearsay evidence is evidence that is told to the witness and not actually seen or heard by the witness themselves. This is not usually admissible in court.
Associated Words: To Admit (verb), Hearsay (noun), Witness (person).

To Allocate (verb): To allocate means to assign or designate and is used in legal English when the court chooses the correct track for a claim to proceed on. In civil litigation there are three choices: small claims court, fast track and multi-track. The court will look at the characteristics of the claim including the amount of damages claimed, the complexity of the issues and the importance of the claim. The parties must complete a document called the 'Directions Questionnaire'. The court will then allocate the claim to a track. Usually, if a claim is complicated or of a large monetary value, the court will allocate the claim to the multi-track. Each track has its own rules for how the claim proceeds.
Associated Words: Allocated (past simple), Allocated (3rd form), Allocation (noun), Claim (noun), Damages (noun), Directions Questionnaire (noun), Small Claims Court (noun), Fast Track (noun), Multi-Track (noun).

Application (noun): In legal English an application is a request for something from the court or other party. The collocation used is "to make an application". For example, an application can be made to the court for further disclosure from another party. Sometimes the court will want to schedule a hearing to hear the arguments in order to make a ruling on the application. The word 'application' is also the name for the document or court form used. There are many different types of application and the correct form must be used to make the right application to the court. There are many rules in the Civil Procedure Rules in relation to time limits and procedure for applications.
Associated Words: To Make an Application (collocation), Civil Procedure Rules (noun), Disclosure (noun), To Hear (verb).

Case Management Conference "CMC" (noun): A case management conference is a hearing in which the issues, timetable and procedure of the claim is organised. For instance, a case management conference can give directions on disclosure of documents, witness statements, expert reports, etc. The CMCs are seen as a very important part of the process, especially with multi-track claims. It is common for the court to schedule a CMC soon after the particulars of claim and defence have been filed in order for the issues to be identified quickly.

Associated Words: Claim (noun), Defence (noun), Disclosure (noun), Expert (person), To File (verb), Hearing (noun), Issues (noun), Multi-Track (noun), Particulars of Claim (noun), Witness Statement (noun).

Conditional Fee Agreement (noun): This is an agreement between a lawyer and their client where it is agreed that a fee is only payable for the lawyer's services if the case results in a favourable conclusion for the client. This means that the lawyer is only paid if the client wins the case or if the claim is settled out of court. The fee is then taken as a percentage of the money won or received in settlement. These agreements are also known as "No-win no-fee" agreements. If the case is lost, the lawyer is not paid for their services.

Associated Words: Case (noun), Claim (noun), To Settle (verb).

Counsel (person): Counsel is an alternative word usually used for a barrister, however, it can also be used for an advocate and so the phrase "counsel for the claimant" means the lawyer representing the claimant.

Associated Words: Barrister (person), Claimant (noun).

Directions (noun): These are orders from the court that must be complied with by the parties. They are usually procedural obligations that the court feel are necessary for the smooth running of the proceedings. Directions can be agreed by the parties by using a consent order, or the parties may have to attend court for a hearing or case management conference for the directions to be ordered by the court. A common collocation is "the court gives the following directions:"

Associated Words: To Direct (verb), To Give Directions (collocation), Case Management Conference (noun), Comply With (phrasal verb), Consent

Order (noun), Hearing (noun), Party (noun), Proceedings (noun).

Directions Questionnaire (noun): This is an official court document that must be completed by the parties to assist the court to decide which track the claim should proceed on.
Associated Words: Claim (noun), Party (noun).

Disclosure (noun): This is the process of stating what documents a party knows exist and are relevant to the claim. This includes stating all the documents which you wish to rely on and, very importantly, all documents that exist but do not help your claim. It is fundamental to the Civil Procedure Rules that each party provides full disclosure of all relevant documents both with documents that assist their case and those that do not. If a party states that a document exists, the other parties may then inspect this document and vice versa. Some documents may exist but do not have to be shown to the court or to other parties. These include documents that are privileged, documents that are marked "without prejudice" or documents that may damage the public interest. The schedule for the full disclosure of documents is usually set out in the case management conference, but disclosure is an ongoing obligation throughout proceedings.
Associated Words: Claim (noun), Case Management Conference (noun), Civil Procedure Rules (noun), Privilege (noun), Without Prejudice (noun).

Fast Track (noun): This is the system used in the Civil Procedure Rules that generally deals with claims that are worth less than £25,000. The concept of the fast track is to deal with these lower value, yet substantial, cases effectively in accordance with the overriding objective. For example, under the fast track the court will try to schedule a final hearing within 30 weeks from the date the case was allocated.
Associated Words: To Allocate (verb), Case (noun), Claim (noun), Civil Procedure Rules (noun), Hearing (noun), Overriding Objective (noun).

To Hear (verb): In legal English this verb means listening to the advocates in court. For example, "the case will be heard next Monday at 12pm". The noun "hearing" is also very common in legal English. It is used when the advocates and judge(s) meet in court to discuss the case. For example, "the

hearing is scheduled for 12th March".
Associated Words: Heard (past simple), Heard (3rd form), Hearing (noun), Advocate (person), Court (noun), Judge (person).

Instructions to Counsel (noun): This is a document drafted by a solicitor to a barrister. It is a request for advice or assistance in relation to a specific question of law or in request for representation of the solicitor's client in court.
Associated Words: To Advise (verb), Barrister (person), To Represent (verb), Solicitor (person).

Jurisdiction (noun): This word is used when a court has the authority or the right to hear and decide cases in that area of law and in that location. In legal English lawyers say that the court "has jurisdiction" to hear the case. For example, the Supreme Court has jurisdiction to hear appeal cases sent from the Court of Appeal in England and Wales. This means that they have the authority or the right to hear these cases.
Associated Words: To have Jurisdiction (collocation), Court (noun), To Hear (verb), Right (noun).

Legal Professional Privilege (noun): This is a right that belongs to a lawyer's client which ensures that communication (letters, etc) that a client has with their lawyer will stay secret and confidential. Usually in litigation proceedings both parties must allow the other party to see all the relevant documents and evidence in the case. However, communication between a client and their lawyer does not have to be given to the other party because it is privileged and so stays confidential. This privilege belongs to the client, not the lawyer and only the client can choose for a privileged document to be shown to the other party. This is called "waiving privilege".
Associated Words: Court (noun), Party (noun), To Waive (verb).

Master (person): This is an official of the High Court of Justice. A Master will sit and hear applications and case management conferences to help organise and schedule timetables for proceedings. It is similar to the role of a judge but they usually deal with procedural matters.
Associated Words: Applications (noun), Case Management Case (noun), To

Hear (verb), Judge (person), Matters (noun), Proceedings (noun), To Sit (verb).

Mediation (noun): This is a popular form of alternative dispute resolution. It is a separate process from litigation and its aim is to settle disputes between parties without the need for further litigation.
Associated Words: Dispute (noun), Parties (noun), To Settle (verb).

Multi-Track (noun): This is the system used in the Civil Procedure Rules for claims worth over £25,000 or for claims that have a high level of complexity or importance. A new multi-track claim will usually have a case management conference to schedule all the necessary steps that all parties must take up to the final hearing.
Associated Words: Case Management Conference (noun), Claim (noun), Civil Procedure Rules (noun), Hearing (noun), Parties (noun).

Part 36 Offer (noun): Part 36 of the Civil Procedure Rules deals with offers to settle. A party can make an offer to settle with or without using Part 36, however, if they choose to use Part 36 then it could help them later if the claim goes to a final hearing. Part 36 offers are confidential between the parties. The court will not know they exist until after judgment has been given. The reason for this is that Part 36 is trying to help the parties settle the case. The concept is, that if a defendant makes a reasonable offer to the claimant before the trial, then the claimant should accept this offer. This is important because if the claimant does not accept a reasonable offer, they will be punished for this when the court decides what percentage of costs the defendant must pay to the claimant. Let's look at an example: During legal proceedings the defendant makes a confidential Part 36 offer to the claimant of £30,000. The claimant rejects the offer and the case continues and goes to trial. At the trial, the judge (who does not know about the Part 36 offer) decides that the defendant is liable and should pay the claimant £20,000. The claimant wins the case, but the amount awarded by the court is less than the defendant's Part 36 offer. The concept here is that the claimant should have accepted the Part 36 offer and should not have continued the claim. The court may then order that the claimant acted unreasonably when they rejected the Part 36 offer and so have to pay their own costs.

Associated Words: Claim (noun), Claimant (noun), Costs (noun), Defendant (noun), Hearing (noun), Liable (adjective), To Offer to Settle (collocation), To Order (verb), To Settle (verb).

Recorder (person): This is an official of the judiciary. They sit as part-time judges in both civil and criminal law systems. There are also Honorary Recorders who are senior judges of certain jurisdictions.
Associated Words: Judge (person), Judiciary (noun), Jurisdiction (noun), To Sit (verb).

Reply to Defence (noun): This is a statement of case that gives the claimant a chance to provide a written response to the defendant's arguments stated in the defence.
Associated Words: Claimant (noun), Defendant (noun), Statement of Case (noun).

Small Claims Court (noun): This is the system that deals with low value proceedings. Usually, if a claimant is claiming less than £10,000 the claim will be allocated to the small claims court. The limit is only a guideline and some cases at higher value will also be allocated to the small claims court if their claim is seen as very simple. The advantage of the small claims court is that there are less procedural obligations for the parties and the claim is dealt with very quickly.
Associated Words: To Allocate (verb), Case (noun), Claim (noun), Claimant (noun), Obligations (noun), Parties (noun).

Stay of Proceedings (noun): This is an order from the court that the proceedings are stopped for a period of time. It is common for claims to be stayed for a certain length of time, but it is also possible for proceedings to be stayed indefinitely. Indefinitely means that there is no specific time limit. Stays are also sometimes known as 'Tomlin Orders', named after the judge who introduced the concept to the courts.
Associated Words: Claim (noun), Order (noun), Proceedings (noun).

Standstill Agreement (noun): This is an agreement when the parties agree to "stop time" so that the limitation period is extended. It is common when certain other investigations or proceedings must conclude before a claim can continue in the courts.

Associated Words: Claim (noun), Limitation Period (noun).

Summary Judgment (noun): This is a judgment from the court that orders that the claimant's case has no real prospect of success or that the defendant has no real prospect of successfully defending the claim. The court will then find in favour of the other party.

Associated Words: Case (noun), Claim (noun), Claimant (noun), To Defend (verb), Defendant (noun), To Find in Favour (collocation), Judgment (noun), To Order (verb), Party (noun).

5 TRIAL

Balance of Probabilities (noun): This is the standard of proof that the claimant must satisfy to be successful in their claim. This means that in civil litigation a claimant must prove their claim is more likely to have happened than not. It is a completely different standard of proof from criminal law, where the standard of proof is to be sure of the guilt of the defendant. This was previously known as beyond reasonable doubt.
Associated Words: Case (noun), Claim (noun), Claimant (noun), Defendant (noun), Standard of Proof (noun).

To Bind (verb): This means that a law, common or statute, must be obeyed and followed by the court. It is used in common law where, for example, a court of first instance must follow the decisions of higher courts. This is called the doctrine of precedent. Rulings or judgments of the higher courts create precedents. These precedents "bind" the lower courts. This means that the lower courts must follow the principles of law set by the higher courts. In legal English it is said that the precedent is "binding", meaning it must be followed.
Associated Words: Bound (past simple), Bound (3rd form), Binding (adjective), To be Bound by Precedent/the Court (collocation), Common Law (noun), Judgment (noun), Precedent (noun).

Closing Statement/Submissions (noun): This is the final part of the advocacy in the trial. Each advocate, for all of the parties in the claim, will give a closing statement to the court. This is also known as making submissions. The advocate will summarise their arguments in an attempt to convince the court to rule in their favour.
Associated Words: Advocate (person), To Give a Closing Statement (collocation), To Make Submissions (collocation), To Rule (verb), To Summarise (verb), Trial (noun).

Consent Order (noun): This is an order from the court that has been agreed in advance by all the parties. Usually, a consent order will agree the procedural aspects of the case that are not in dispute.
Associated Words: Case (noun), Dispute (noun), Order (noun), Parties

(noun).

Contempt of Court (noun): If a person or organisation does not comply with or obey the rules and orders of the court, then they will be held in contempt of court. It is usually used in relation to the parties' behaviour in court but also it is used to ensure that any media reporting of cases is complicit with the rules and regulations of the court.
Associated Words: To be Held in Contempt of Court (collocation), To Comply With (phrasal verb), To Obey (verb), Order (noun), Party (noun).

Cross-Examination (noun): This means that an advocate asks questions to a witness from another party in the claim. For example, Mr Robinson sues Mr Dibbs. In court Mr Robinson's advocate (a barrister or a solicitor) will first ask Mr Robinson questions about his claim. This is called examination-in-chief. After these questions, Mr Dibbs' advocate will ask Mr Robinson questions about his claim. This is called cross-examination. Later, Mr Robinson's advocate will get a chance to cross-examine Mr Dibbs and his witnesses.
Associated Words: Advocate (person), Barrister (noun), Claim (noun), Party (noun), Solicitor (noun), To Sue (verb).

To Examine (verb): This means to ask questions in court. There are three main types: examination-in-chief, cross-examination and re-examination.
Associated Words: Examined (past simple), Examined (3rd form), Cross-examination (noun), Examination (noun).

Examination-in-Chief (noun): This is the process of an advocate asking questions to their client and their witnesses in court. After a witness is examined by their own advocate, the witness is then cross-examined by opposing advocates.
Associated Words: Advocate (person), Cross-examine (verb), Witness (person).

Expert Witness (person): This is a person who the court believes can assist proceedings because of their specialist knowledge on a particular subject. For instance, psychologists, accountants and childcare workers are examples of

expert witnesses.
Associated Words: Party (noun), Proceedings (noun).

To Give Judgment (collocation): This means that the judge(s) have made a decision and are ready to give their reasons for the decision. These reasons for the decision come in the form of a judgment. The collocation to give judgment means that the judge reads the reasoning behind the decision to the parties in court.
Associated Words: Gave judgment (past simple), Given Judgment (3rd form), Judge (person).

To Grant (verb): In legal English this means that something is given or allowed to happen. For instance, if a party requests the chance to appeal a judgment, the court may agree and so will 'grant' leave to appeal. This means that it gives the party permission to appeal the judgment.
Associated Words: Granted (past simple), Granted (3rd form), To Appeal (verb), Judgment (noun), Party (noun).

Leave (noun): This word means permission to do something. In legal English it is used when the court permits a party to appeal a judgment or allows an application to be made to appeal.
Associated Words: To Appeal (verb), Application (noun), Judgment (noun), Party (noun).

Liable (adjective): This means that a party is legally responsible for their actions or omissions. Omissions means that a party did not do something that they should have done. If a party is liable then the court will usually order the liable party to remedy the damage or problem. This can be with money, known as damages, or action, known as an injunction.
Associated Words: Damages (noun), Injunction (noun), Party (noun).

Opening Statement (noun): This is the first speech by the advocate in court. An advocate will usually use this opportunity to explain to the court what the basis of his client's argument and position is. Each party will have a chance to give an opening statement to the court. Once this has been completed by all parties, the evidential part of the trial with the examination of witnesses will begin.

Associated Words: Advocate (person), Evidence (noun), To Examine (verb), Party (noun), Witness (person).

Precedent (noun): This meaning of the word precedent is in relation to common law. Historically, judgments of the courts were written down, also known as "recorded". Over the centuries that followed, a system of following the decisions of the higher courts became usual practice. Nowadays the system of following precedent is one of the most important doctrines of the English legal system. The process is fairly simple. The judgments of the higher courts (Supreme Court and Court of Appeal) must be followed by the lower courts (High Court, County Court, etc). For example, if there is a case about a dispute over a point of law, the lawyers will check the records of the Supreme Court and the Court of Appeal to see if there is a ruling from these courts that will tell them what was decided in similar cases before. If the facts and situations of the cases are very similar then the court must follow this precedent. If the facts and situation are not so similar then the court does not have to follow the precedent. Each judgment will have a part called the "ratio decidendi". This is the part of the judgment which forms the precedent and the part that should be followed by the lower courts. This is the doctrine of "binding precedents". **Associated Words:** To Bind (verb), Court of Appeal (noun), County Court (noun), High Court (noun), Judgment (noun), Ratio Decidendi (noun), Supreme Court (noun).

Re-examination (noun): This means that an advocate may ask his client and their witnesses more questions after the opposing advocates have completed their cross-examination. The advocate may only ask questions relating to issues that were raised during cross-examination by the opposing advocates.

Associated Words: Advocate (person), Cross-examination (noun), Witness (person).

Reserve Judgment (noun): This means that the judge(s) decide to spend more time considering their decision. The judges will usually tell the parties at the end of the trial that they wish to reserve judgment and will notify the parties when they have reached a verdict. There are no rules for the time limits but the length of time usually depends on the length and complexity of the case.

Associated Words: Judge (person), Parties (noun), Verdict (noun).

To Seek (verb): In normal everyday English, this verb means to look for something, however, in legal English it is used by advocate to ask the court to make an order or to find in their favour. Common collocations are "to seek an order from the court", or " to seek judgment in the (claimant's) favour".

Associated Words: Sought (past simple), Sought (3rd form), Judgment (noun), Order (noun).

Summons (noun): This is a document from the court that orders a person to attend court to give evidence or to produce an exhibit or document.

Associated Words: Evidence (noun), Exhibit (noun), To Order (verb).

Verdict (noun): This means the decision of the judge or court.

Associated Words: Judge (person), To Reach a Verdict (collocation).

Witness (person): This is a person who can assist the court with a claim. A witness can be an actual witness, known as an eye-witness, an expert witness or someone who knows something in relation to the claim and can help the court reach its verdict.

Associated Words: Claim (noun), Expert (person), To Reach a Verdict (collocation).

6 AFTER THE TRIAL

To Appeal (verb): To appeal means to ask a higher court or tribunal to review a decision or judgment to reverse or overrule part or all of it. There are many reasons why a judgment is appealed. For example, it could be appealed because the judge(s) made a mistake with the law or because new evidence has appeared in the case. The process for appealing is simple. Usually, a special application or request is made to the court. In some cases permission (or "leave") of the court must be obtained to allow the application. If the appeal is allowed, the appellate court will hear the case again. The party who applies for the appeal is called the appellant and the other party is called the respondent. A common collocation used in legal English is "appeal against the judgment/verdict/decision")

Associated Words: Appealed (past simple), Appealed (3rd form), Appealed (adjective), Appeal (noun), To Appeal against something (collocation), Appellant (noun), Appellate Court (noun), Court (noun), Evidence (noun), To Hear (verb), Judgment (noun), Party (noun), Respondent (noun).

Appellant (noun): This is a party who appeals against a verdict or decision of a court or tribunal.

Associated Words: To Appeal (verb), To Appeal against something (collocation), Party (noun), Verdict (noun).

Attachment of Earnings Order (noun): This is a ruling from the court that orders the defendant to pay a judgment debt directly from their salary or wages. The court will usually order that a percentage of the defendant's salary will automatically be transferred to the claimant every week or every month.

Associated Words: Debt (noun), Defendant (noun), Judgment Debt (noun), To Order (verb).

To Award (verb): This verb is used when the court grants a remedy to a party in the claim. An example of a common collocation is "the court awarded the claimant £50,000 in damages".

Associated Words: Claim (noun), Claimant (noun), Damages (noun), To Grant (verb), Remedy (noun).

Bailiff (person): This is a person who has authority from the court to collect unpaid judgment debts. The bailiff collects money or property owned by the defendant which can then be sold for the equal amount of the debt.
Associated Words: Debt (noun), Judgment (noun).

Bankruptcy (noun): This word is very common in the English legal system and describes the situation when the court declares that an individual, sole trader or partnership does not have enough money to pay its debts. This term is commonly misunderstood with the term insolvency. If you do not have enough money to pay all your debts, you are insolvent. You are not bankrupt until the court officially declares that you are unable to pay all your debts. Also, the term bankruptcy is used in England and Wales only in relation to individuals, sole traders and partnerships. The term is not used in relation to companies in England and Wales.
Associated Words: Bankrupt (adjective), To Go Bankrupt (collocation), To Be Declared Bankrupt by the Court (collocation).

Charge (noun): This is a legal right that one party has over the property or assets of another party. It is used when one party does not have enough money to pay a judgment debt. For example, the court finds in favour of the claimant and awards the claimant £50,000 in damages. The defendant submits that they do not have £50,000, but they do own a house. The court can order that a charge is put on the defendant's property to the value of £50,000 in favour of the claimant. This means that when the defendant sells the house, the claimant will be paid £50,000 from the money of the sale. The money from the sale of a house is called the proceeds of sale.
Associated Words: Claimant (noun), Debt (noun), Defendant (noun), In Favour Of (collocation), Judgment (noun), Order (noun).

To Comply With (phrasal verb): This means to obey or follow a request. It is used in relation to judgments and orders. A party must comply with a court order, for example to pay damages to the other party or to comply with an injunction.
Associated Words: Damages (noun), Injunction (noun), Judgment (noun), Order (noun), Party (noun).

Compound Interest (noun): This is money that must be paid in addition to judgment debt interest. Usually, if the claimant is successful, damages are awarded plus interest. Interest is calculated as a percentage of the damages. If the defendant does not pay the damages to the defendant on time, the interest rate increases to a higher rate. This higher rate of interest is called compound interest. It is used as financial punishment for the late or non-payment of a judgment debt. For example, the court finds Mr Green liable and awards Mrs Brown £15,000 in damages plus interest at 6%. If Mr Green does not pay the damages to Mrs Brown on time, then the interest rate will increase to 10% for the amount that is paid late. The interest charged at 10% is the compound interest. It is only applied to the payments Mr Green does not pay on time to Mrs Brown.

Associated Words: To Award (verb), Claimant (noun), Damages (noun), Debt (noun), Defendant (noun), Interest (noun), Judgment (noun).

Consequential Loss (noun): This is indirect loss suffered by the defendant. For instance, Miss Anderson causes a bad car accident in which Miss Wright was badly injured. Miss Wright may claim damages for the "direct" loss suffered such as medical bills and repairs to her car. However, she may also claim for "indirect loss" such as loss of salary if she has to take time off work. The loss of salary is a "consequence" of the accident and so this type of loss is called consequential loss. The concept arose from common law in England and Wales.

Associated Words: To Claim (verb), Common Law (noun), Damages (noun), Loss (noun), To Suffer (verb).

Costs (noun): This means the cost of bringing and hearing legal proceedings. In legal English it usually means the fees of the court, barristers, solicitors and the experts who charge for their services. It is a very important concept in legal English as the usual rule is that the party who is unsuccessful must pay the costs of the successful party. In many smaller cases the costs are easily dealt with by the court. This is called a summary assessment. However, in more complicated claims there will be a separate hearing on the issue of costs and an independent expert is appointed to calculate the costs of the parties. This is called a detailed assessment. The Civil Procedure Rules provides guidelines on the rules of costs in proceedings, but it is a very complicated and constantly changing area of law.

Associated Words: Barrister (person), Civil Procedure Rules (noun), Detailed Assessment (noun), Expert (person), Proceedings (noun), Solicitor (person).

Costs on an Indemnity Basis (collocation): This means that the court orders the losing party to pay a high percentage of the winning party's costs.
Associated Words: Case (noun), Costs (noun), Party (noun), Verdict (noun).

Costs on a Standard Basis (collocation): This means the court orders the losing party to pay a reasonable percentage of the winning party's costs.
Associated Words: Case (noun), Costs (noun), Party (noun), Verdict (noun).

Damages (noun): This is the legal English word for compensation or money paid by the liable party to the successful party. Please note that this noun is already plural and does not have a singular form. The noun "damage" means broken and is not a legal English term. Accordingly, the two words, damage and damages are completely different and should not be confused. Damages are a very important concept of civil litigation and this is the most common remedy awarded by the courts.
Associated Words: Liable (noun), Party (noun), Remedy (noun).

Declaration (noun): This is a judgment or award from the court that states a party's rights or legal relationships with other parties. This type of judgment is commonly known as a declaratory judgment.
Associated Words: Award (noun), Judgment (noun).

Detailed Assessment (noun): This is a special procedure where a court will investigate the costs of proceedings to determine whether they are proportionate to the case and how much the unsuccessful party must pay to the successful party.
Associated Words: Costs (noun), Party (noun).

To Enforce (verb): This verb means to make sure that a person or organisation does what they have been ordered to do. The best example of a common collocation in legal English is that a judgment is enforced. This means that the court has authority to force or make sure that the judgment is effective and that all court orders have been complied with. For example, Mr Ball issues a claim against Mrs Clark for £10,000. Mr Ball wins his claim and so the court orders that Mrs Clark must pay £10,000 (plus interest) to Mr Ball in damages. The court gives Mrs Clark 60 days to pay the sum in full. If she does not pay within 60 days, Mr Ball can enforce the judgment. This means he has the right to ask the court to force Mrs Clark to pay the money. This can include asking for a legal charge over property or using the services of a bailiff.

Associated Words: Charge (noun), Claim (noun), Judgment (noun), Order (noun).

To Find (verb): In legal English this verb means to decide or conclude. For instance, the court will "find in favour of the claimant" or "find that a witness is not credible".

Associated Words: Found (past simple), Found (3rd form), Case (noun), Claimant (noun), To Find in Favour (collocation), Witness (person).

To Find in Favour (collocation): This collocation means that the judge(s) have reached a decision and that one of the parties has won the case. Judges(s) can find in favour of either party (the claimant or the defendant) and in both of these situations the collocation to find in favour can be used.

Associated Words: Found in Favour (past simple), Found in Favour (3rd form), Case (noun), Claimant (noun), Defendant (noun), Judge (person), Party (noun).

Freezing Order (noun): This is an order of the court that stops a party to the proceedings from transferring their assets, usually money in a bank account, out of the jurisdiction of the court. It is usually ordered to stop potential problems in relation to the payment of the judgment debts. It is also known as a Mareva Order or a Mareva Injunction.

Associated Words: Debt (noun), Injunction (noun), Judgment (noun), Jurisdiction (noun), Order (noun), Party (noun), Proceedings (noun).

Injunction (noun): This is a type of remedy available from the court. An injunction is an order from the court that states that a party must do something, or stop from doing something. A party who does not follow or obey an injunction can be liable in both criminal and civil law and can face serious penalties if they do not comply with the injunction.

Associated Words: To Comply With (collocation), Order (noun), Party (noun), Remedy (noun).

Interest (noun): This means extra money that can be claimed in addition to damages. It is usually a percentage of the amount of damages claimed.

Associated Word: Damages (noun).

Joint and Several Liability (collocation): This phrase means that if there is a group of two or more people who are liable for a judgment debt, then all of the members of the group are liable individually and also together as a group. For example, if Mr and Mrs Benson are liable for damages, the court may order that the liability is joint and several. This means that Mr Smith is liable for all of the debt, Mrs Smith is liable for all the debt, and together Mr and Mrs Smith are liable for the debt. The court can enforce the judgment against both Mr and Mrs Benson individually or together.

Associated Words: Damages (noun), To Enforce (verb), Liable (noun), To Order (verb).

Judgment Debt (noun): A debt is money owed by one person or organisation to another. A judgment debt is money that must be paid by a party to another party by order of the court.

Associated Words: Debt (noun), Judgment (noun), Order (noun), Party (noun).

Loss (noun): This means the reduction in value of something that has been damaged, broken or injured. It is a very important concept in civil litigation and dispute resolution, as loss must be suffered for compensation to be paid. It is the basis of claims in both tort and contract law and must be established before the court for a claim to be successful.

Associated Words: Claim (noun), Contract Law (noun), Dispute Resolution (noun), Litigation (noun), To Suffer (verb).

Obligation (noun): An obligation is something that a person must do. An obligation can be legal or moral but within the English legal system it is common to see the words "duties and obligations" especially in commercial contracts. This means that the parties to the contract must do (or must not do) whatever is written in this section of the contract. In legal English the phrase "to fulfil an obligation" is very common. To fulfil an obligation means to complete it.

Associated Words: Contract Law (noun), To Fulfil an Obligation (collocation), Party (noun).

To Order (verb): This means that the court states that something must be done, stopped or prohibited from being done. The noun "order" is the document used to state the orders of the court. The collocation used is "to make an order".

Associated Words: Ordered (past simple), Ordered (3rd form), Order (noun), To Make an Order (collocation).

Remedy (noun): This word is used to describe the way a court will try to compensate or resolve the harm or loss that the claimant has suffered. There are three main types of remedy in civil litigation. The most common is damages. This is monetary compensation awarded to the claimant to compensate them for their loss. The second, called equitable remedies, are injunctions and specific performance. These are court orders that specify that a particular action must be taken or is prohibited. The third are declaratory judgments which state the rights or legal relationships between parties.

Associated Words: To Remedy (verb), Claimant (noun), Damages (noun), Declaratory Judgment (noun), Equitable (noun), Harm (noun), Injunction (noun), Loss (noun), To Order (verb), Specific Performance (noun).

Remoteness (noun): Remoteness is a concept in relation to damages. Common law states that damages can only be awarded to an injured party where the loss was not too remote. This means that the loss suffered must be within the reasonable contemplation of the parties. This means that the loss suffered must be reasonably predictable at the time of the breach. The rule is used to stop claims where claimants are unreasonable in the amount and the reasons for their claim.

Associated Words: To Award (verb), Claim (noun), Claimant (noun), Common Law (noun), Damages (noun), Injured Party (noun), Party (noun), To Suffer (verb).

To Rescind (verb): This verb is used as a remedy to cancel a contract between parties. The principle of the remedy is to put all the parties back in the position they were in before they entered into the contract. In England and Wales, the court has the power to rescind a contract in certain situations. **Associated Words:** Party (noun), Remedy (noun).

Respondent (noun): This is a party who is served an appeal notice by an appellant and, accordingly, must respond to the notice. **Associated Words:** To Appeal (verb), Party (noun).

Restitution (noun): This is a type of remedy from the court. Usually the court will order compensation to be paid by the defendant for the loss suffered by the claimant in the form of damages. However, in some situations the loss suffered by the claimant may be very small. The court has the option to order restitution. The law of restitution means that the court orders the defendant to pay their profits that resulted from their breach of contract to the claimant. For example, Mr Burgess issues proceedings against Mr Shaw for breach of contract. Mr Burgess did not actually suffer any loss as a result of Mr Shaw's breach, but if Mr Shaw profited greatly from the result of his breach, then the court can order restitution and order that Mr Shaw pay his profits from his breach of contract to Mr Burgess. **Associated Words:** To Breach (verb), Claimant (noun), Damages (noun), Defendant (noun), Loss (noun), To Order (verb), Remedy (noun), To Suffer (verb).

Search Order (noun): This is a court order that states that a property can be searched and evidence seized without warning. Seized means that the property is taken and held in a safe place by the authorities. Clearly, this order is only used in the most exceptional and serious situations. For example, the court will order a search order (or warrant) when the court believes there is a danger that evidence will be destroyed by the defendant. This order was previously known as an Anton Piller order as it was named after a case of the

same name.
Associated Words: Evidence (noun), Order (noun).

Specific Performance (noun): This is a remedy from the court that orders a party to do a certain act. Usually specific performance is ordered to make a party fulfil their obligations under a contract. It is an alternative remedy when damages are perhaps not relevant to the claim as the claimant has not actually suffered any loss.
Associated Words: Claim (noun), Claimant (noun), Damages (noun), To Fulfil an Obligation (collocation), Loss (noun), To Order (verb), Remedy (noun), To Suffer (verb).

Summary Assessment (noun): This is a special procedure when the court will deal with the costs of the case fairly quickly and without the need for costs proceedings or detailed assessment of costs. Summary assessment is common for lower value, simple claims.
Associated Words: Claim (noun), Costs (noun), Detailed Assessment (noun).

Vexatious Litigation (noun): This means that a claimant issues a number of claims that are totally without merit. Without merit means that there are no grounds or good reasons to make the claim. Vexatious litigants are usually placed on a special list and must ask the court for permission to issue a claim with the court. The courts are generally reluctant to place a litigant on the list as it restricts their access to the courts. It is, therefore, not common for litigants to be placed on the list without good reason.
Associated Words: Claim (noun), Claimant (noun), Grounds (noun), To Issue a Claim (collocation).

Warrant of Execution (noun): This is a court document that grants permission to a bailiff to collect a judgment debt. This may include entering a debtor's property and taking their possessions. These possessions are then sold to collect money to pay the judgment debt.
Associated Words: Bailiff (person), Debt (noun), To Grant (verb), Judgment Debt (noun)

7 TYPES OF PROCEEDINGS AND CLAIMS

Breach of Contract (noun): The verb "to breach" is the legal term that means to break. If there is a breach of contract it means that one party to the contract has not fulfiled their obligations under that contract. In other words, they have "broken" the contract. As a result of this, the injured party may bring proceedings for breach of contract. These types of claims are very common in civil litigation and dispute resolution and cover many different areas of law.
Associated Words: Claim (noun), Dispute (noun), To Fulfil an Obligation (collocation), Injured Party (noun), Proceedings (noun).

Copyright/Trademark/Patent Infringement (noun): This means that a piece of work (book, music, film, etc) has been used without the permission of the owner of the work. Copyright infringement can include copying, publishing, re-producing or re-selling. Other more informal terms for copyright infringement are "piracy" and "copyright theft".
Associated Word: To Infringe (verb).

Defamation (noun): This is the name of the area of law that deals with false, negative statements. Defamation is the communication of a statement made by somebody about somebody else which causes this person to have a negative or worse image or reputation. Defamation can be divided into two areas: slander and libel.
Associated Words: Slander (noun), Libel (noun).

Discrimination (noun): These are proceedings brought by an individual or organisation that means that they believe that they have been treated in a worse way than other people. Common claims for discrimination include racial, gender, religious, age, sexual orientation and disability.
Associated Words: Claim (noun), Proceedings (noun).

Divorce (noun): This means that a married couple do not wish to continue living their lives together in a legal relationship. A divorce is a legal agreement to end the marriage and decides future arrangements in relation to children, property, money and other assets that the couple own. In legal English a married couple "get a divorce" or "get divorced". This agreement must be accepted and approved by the court.

Associated Words: To Divorce (verb), To Get a Divorce (collocation), To Get Divorced (collocation), Court (noun).

Group Litigation (noun): Group litigation is the name for proceedings which have many parties. In this situation the Civil Procedure Rules allow the court to make a Group Litigation Order ("GLO"). A GLO allows all the claimants to bring the claim together as one main claim. These proceedings are usually on a large scale and so involve case management conferences to organise and schedule the obligations of the parties. A lead solicitor is usually appointed to run and manage the GLO.

Associated Words: Claim (noun), Claimant (noun), Civil Procedure Rules (noun), Party (noun), Proceedings (noun).

Harassment (noun): This means that one person or a group of people are acting in an unpleasant, threatening or disturbing way. To threaten means to force someone to do something that they do not want to do and if they do not do it then they will be punished. In civil litigation and dispute resolution, harassment usually happens in two main areas. The first area is at work and is covered by employment law, the second is sexual harassment which is also a criminal offence. An important thing to note in legal English is that in some countries the term "mobbing" is used to describe harassment. Please be careful if you wish to use this term as it is not common in legal English in this context.

Associated Words: Dispute Resolution (noun).

Human Rights (noun): Due to the European Convention on Human Rights and the Human Rights Act 1998, these claims have become increasingly popular in in the English courts. Common claims are brought regarding freedom of speech, right to a fair trial, freedom of religion and freedom of movement and establishment.

Associated Word: Claim (noun).

Insolvency Proceedings (noun): These proceedings are for situations when a company, organisation or individual cannot pay all of their debts. There are a number of options available depending on the specific circumstances of the case, however, commonly the phrase "winding up" is used in legal English to describe the process for companies.
Associated Words: Case (noun), Debt (noun).

Libel (noun): This is a type of defamation. Libel is the written or broadcast communication of a false statement that makes a person or organisation's reputation or image worsen.
Associated Word: Defamation (noun).

Misrepresentation (noun): This is a claim that means that one party persuaded another party to enter into a contract by making false statements about the contract. For instance, Mr Craig wants to buy Mrs Robinson's car. Mrs Robinson tells Mr Craig that her car is 5 years old and has travelled 50,000 kilometers. Mr Craig buys the car but it stops working after one month. Later Mr Craig discovers that the car is actually 10 years old and has travelled 100,000 kilometers. Due to these false statements, Mr Craig can bring a claim against Mrs Robinson for misrepresentation.
Associated Words: To Bring a Claim (collocation).

Negligence (noun): This is a very common type of legal proceeding and means that a party has failed to act in the same way that a reasonable person would do and that this failure caused another person harm or loss. It is similar to the non-legal term "carelessness". It is a large and complex area of law which is governed mostly by common law, although there is some statutory legislation on the subject. To establish negligence a claimant must first show that the defendant owed them a duty of care, second that the defendant breached that duty of care and, third that the breach resulted in the claimant suffering loss. If the claimant can prove all three aspects, then the defendant may be held liable by the court and ordered to pay damages to the claimant. An interesting principle from negligence is that there does not need to be any prior relationship or contract between the parties for a duty of care to be established.
Associated Words: Negligent (adjective), To Breach (verb), Claimant

(noun), Damages (noun), Defendant (noun), Duty of Care (noun), Harm (noun), Loss (noun), To Suffer (verb).

Nuisance (noun): This is a common law tort that affects a person's quiet enjoyment of their property. A claim for nuisance can be brought for an action that disturbs or annoys another person, such as loud noise, pollution, dangerous chemicals, etc. The common law remedy for nuisance is damages, but under the law of equity, injunctions are also available from the court.
Associated Words: Claim (noun), Damages (noun), Equity (noun), Injunction (noun), Remedy (noun), Tort (noun).

Personal Injury (noun): This area of law deals with physical suffering. One of the most common negligence claims are for personal injury where a negligent act or omission has caused physical harm. It is a well-established and a large area of civil litigation. Also, the Civil Procedure Rules has a specific pre-action protocol for these types of claims.
Associated Words: To Cause (verb), Claim (noun), Civil Procedure Rules (noun), Harm (noun), Negligence (noun).

Product Liability (noun): This area of law deals with the situation when a person or business buys a defective product. Defective means that the product is broken or is not fit or safe to use. Product liability is an area of law that helps the consumer if they buy something that is not working or does not do what it should. For a product liability claim, a claimant does not need to establish negligence or intention because this tort is a "strict liability" tort.
Associated Words: Harm (noun), Loss (noun), Negligence (noun), Strict Liability (noun), To Suffer (verb), Tort (noun).

Professional Negligence (noun): This is a type of claim in civil litigation. This means that a person who has a special skill or trade is negligent in the way they practice that skill or trade. There is not a specific definition of who is a professional and who is not in legal English. There are specific rules for these types of claims and there is a pre-action protocol in the Civil Procedure Rules that must be followed. These claims are usually brought by clients of specialised workers and such claims can be brought in tort or as a breach of contract.

Associated Words: Breach of Contract (noun), Civil Procedure Rules (noun), Claim (noun), Negligence (noun), To Practice (verb), Tort (noun).

Slander (noun): Slander is one of two types of defamation. Slander generally deals with the spoken communication of a false statement about a person or organisation that creates a worse or negative image or reputation.
Associated Word: Defamation (noun).

Strict Liability (noun): This means that a defendant is legally responsible for damage or loss caused by an act or omission, without the claimant having to prove negligence or intention. Torts such as product liability and some crimes, for instance driving under the influence of alcohol are examples of strict liability.
Associated Words: Claimant (noun), Loss (noun), Negligence (noun), Tort (noun).

Tort Law/The Law of Tort (noun): The law of tort relates to "civil wrongs". It is unique in nature as you do not need to have a contract with someone for the law of tort to operate. In the law of tort there are situations when we owe a duty of care to other people, even to people who we have never met before. In these situations we must be careful not to cause or create any injury or damage in these situations. It is a very complicated and ever-changing area of law and there are thousands of common law cases and precedents that have developed the law of Tort over hundreds of years. Tort law includes negligence (carelessness), nuisance (stopping someone having quiet enjoyment of their home), defamation (slander and libel), false imprisonment and trespass (to land and to the person). It is a common law principle and is designed to compensate the victim. It was not initially designed to punish the person who caused the tort (also known as a "tortfeasor").
Associated Words: Common Law (noun), Defamation (noun), Libel (noun), Negligence (noun), Nuisance (noun), Slander (noun), Precedent (noun).

Trespass (noun): This is a type of tort which can be divided into three parts. The first part is trespass to land which means that somebody is interfering

with land or property that they do not own and do not have any rights over. To interfere means that somebody is affecting something in a negative way. For example, if I park my car on my neighbour's garden without permission, I am trespassing. The second type of trespass is trespass to the person. This is unwanted interference with another person. More commonly, trespass to the person is known as battery or assault depending on the act. False imprisonment is also trespass to the person and means that somebody does not allow another person the freedom to move or go where or when they wish to. The third type of trespass is trespass to chattels. Chattels means goods, property or more informally, things. Recently in legal English, trespass to chattels has developed to include claims in respect of spam email and internet server interference.
Associated Words: Claim (noun), Tort (noun).

Unfair Dismissal (noun): This means that an employee's employment contract is terminated without fair grounds or reasons. The employee would bring a claim for unfair dismissal to compensate them for the suffering and loss suffered as a result of the dismissal.
Associated Words: Claim (noun), Grounds (noun), Loss (noun), To Suffer (verb).

Wills and Probate (noun): This is the procedure for distributing the assets and possessions of a person who has died. A will is a document that states the intentions of the person who died. Usually, there is not a dispute in relation to the distribution of a will, however, sometimes the will is contested by the beneficiaries. A beneficiary is a person who receives money or property from the will. If a will is contested, this means that two or more people disagree with the will or the circumstances under which the will was written. Proceedings are then brought to resolve these types of disputes before the courts.
Associated Words: Beneficiary (noun), Dispute (noun), Proceedings (noun), To Resolve (verb).

8 GLOSSARY

Before a Claim

Adjudication
To Allege
Alternative Dispute Resolution
Arbitration
To Breach
Causation
Carelessness
Civil Procedure Rules
To Commit
To Dispute
Duty of Care
Foreseeable
Governing Law
Grounds
To Harm
To Infringe
Injured Party
Letter Before Action
Litigation
Loss
To Omit
Overriding Objective
Practice Direction
Pre-action Protocol
To Resolve
To Settle
To Suffer
Woolf Report

Making a Claim

Affidavit
Barrister
To Brief
To Bring an Action
Burden of Proof
Case
To Claim
Claimant
Claim Form
Court Fee
Evidence
Exhibit
To File
To Issue
Issue
Limitation
Litigant in Person
Particulars of Claim
Plaintiff
To Plead
Proceedings
To Serve
Solicitor
Statement of Case
Statement of Truth
To Submit
Third Party

Defending a Claim

Acknowledgement of service
To Admit
Contributory Negligence

To Counterclaim
Default Judgment
To Defend
To Deny
Mitigation of Loss
To Respond

Court Proceedings

Admissible
To Allocate
Application
Case Management Conference
Conditional Fee Agreement
Counsel
Directions
Directions Questionnaire
Disclosure
Fast Track
To Hear
Instructions to Counsel
Jurisdiction
Legal Professional Privilege
Master
Mediation
Multi-Track
Part 36 Offer
Recorder
Reply to Defence
Small Claims Court
Stay of Proceedings
Standstill Agreement
Summary Judgment

Trial

Balance of Probabilities
To Bind
Closing Statement/Submissions
Consent Order
Contempt of Court
Cross-examination
To Examine
Examination-in-Chief
Expert Witness
To Give Judgment
To Grant
Leave
Liable
Opening statement
Precedent
Re-examination
Reserve Judgment
To Seek
Summons
Verdict
Witness

After the Trial

To Appeal
Appellant
Attachment of Earnings Order
To Award
Bailiff
Bankruptcy
Charge
To Comply With
Compound Interest

Consequential Loss
Costs
Costs on an Indemnity Basis
Costs on a Standard Basis
Damages
Declaration
Detailed Assessment
To Enforce
To Find
To Find in Favour
Freezing Order
Injunction
Interest
Joint and Several Liability
Judgment Debt
Loss
Obligation
To Order
Remedy
Remoteness
To Rescind
Respondent
Restitution
Search Order
Specific Performance
Summary Assessment
Vexatious Litigation
Warrant of Execution

Types of Proceedings and Claims

Breach of Contract
Copyright/Trademark/Patent Infringement
Defamation
Discrimination
Divorce

Group Litigation
Harassment
Human Rights
Insolvency Proceedings
Libel
Misrepresentation
Negligence
Nuisance
Personal Injury
Product Liability
Professional Negligence
Slander
Strict Liability
Tort
Trespass
Unfair Dismissal
Wills and Probate

DISPUTE RESOLUTION AND LITIGATION

9 EXERCISES

TRUE OR FALSE

Decide if these sentences are true or false (answers are at the back of the book):

1. To commit is the correct verb to use in legal English when stating that a person has done something criminal or tortious.

2. A dispute is a term lawyers use for an argument or disagreement in legal proceedings.

3. Some types of claims have a pre-action protocol in the Civil Procedure Rules. This is for guidance only and parties do not have to follow it.

4. In a civil claim the claimant has the burden of proof. This means that they must show the court that their version of events is more likely that the defendant's version.

5. If the claim is complicated, legal proceedings can be issued directly at the Supreme Court.

6. The main objective of the Civil Procedure Rules is to ensure a fast, inexpensive and fair legal system in the courts. The rules are not designed for claims to settle before legal proceedings begin.

7. To admit liability means that you state you are not legally responsible for what the claimant has alleged.

8. It is common for defendants to file an acknowledgement of service in response to a claim form as it gives them more time to reply to the allegations.

9. All parties have to disclose evidence that is relevant to the claim. This includes evidence that does not assist their case or position.

10. A claim in the small claims court will usually have a case management conference. This organises a schedule of obligations for the parties to comply with.

11. In legal English, jurisdiction means that the court has geographical and authoritative power to hear the claim.

12. A consent order is an order from the court that all the parties have agreed for the court to approve.

13. In civil litigation, a judgment from the Court of Appeal can be appealed to the High Court of Justice.

14. A closing statement is made after all the evidence has been heard by the court.

15. A claim can be issued at any time. There is no limitation period that exists for civil claims.

16. On a claim form, the claimant can state the amount they are claiming in damages plus interest.

17. Restitution is when both parties are put back into the position they would have been in if the contract had not existed. It is a common law remedy.

18. If a claim is for less than £10,000 and is a very simple case, then the claim will probably be allocated to the fast track.

19. A person who issues lots of claims for little or no reason is called a vexatious litigant.

20. If there are many claimants and defendants in the same dispute, all the claims must be issued and heard individually.

VOCABULARY GAP FILL

Complete the sentences with the missing word or phrase (answers are at the back of the book):

1. The legal English term for monetary compensation is _____.

2. To _____ is the verb used to state that the claimant thinks or believes that the defendant committed a breach, but without it being proven in a court of law.

3. My client came to me in relation to a negligence claim. He wanted to issue proceedings immediately, but I advised him that first we need to send a _____ _____ _____ to the defendant stating the grounds of our claim.

4. The main purpose of the Civil Procedure Rules is known as the _____ _____. It is the spirit in which the parties should act in the proceedings.

5. The party that brings a claim is formally called a _____.

6. Counsel will be here in 15 minutes. Our solicitor will _____ her about the latest developments in the case before the hearing begins.

7. The defendant arrived at court without a legal representative. He conducted the hearing as a _____ _____ _____.

8. The defendant was surprised to receive the claim form in the post. He did not agree that he was in breach of contract and so decided to _____ the claim in full.

9. To _____ means to agree or accept that you are responsible for doing something, usually in a negative context.

10. During multi-track proceedings it is very common for the parties to make _____ to the court. These can be for specific reasons such as summary judgment, specific disclosure requests or to strike out the claim.

11. The _____ exercise is one of the most important parts of civil litigation proceedings. The Civil Procedure Rules state that all parties must states which documents they have in their possession.

12. The track which deals with higher value and more complicated claims is called the _____-_____.

13. An example of _____-_____ is the when defendant's lawyer asks questions to the claimant's witness.

14. In legal English, to be _____ means to be legally responsible for your acts or omissions.

15. After all parties have submitted their case to court, the judge will consider their _____ and will give judgment in the next two weeks.

16. The collocation used in legal English when the court gives damages to a claimant is to _____ damages.

17. It is a principle of English law that the claimant must _____ their loss. This means that they must try to keep their loss as low as reasonably possible.

18. If a married couple no longer wish to remain together, the legal collocation is that they _____ _____.

19. The legal term that means to "break" a contract is to _____.

20. Race, religion, age, sex, disability and sexual orientation are example of _____ claims.

PREPOSITION GAP FILL

Complete the sentences using the correct preposition (answers are at the back of the book):

1. The claimant issued a claim against the defendant _____ the grounds of nuisance.

2. To establish negligence under English law, there are a number of tests to satisfy. The first is to establish that the defendant owed the claimant a duty _____ care.

3. It is common for employees to bring _____ action for unfair dismissal against their ex-employers.

4. A claimant must issue a claim form with the court to start proceedings. If the facts or case are complicated, then the claimant can also file particulars _____ claim to set out the claim in detail.

5. One of the most important tasks for a claimant is to serve the claim form _____ the defendant.

6. If the defendant needs more time to respond to the claim then they can file an acknowledgement _____ service.

7. After receiving the claim form the defendant is given a limited amount of time in which to respond _____ the allegations made by the claimant.

8. It is common for the court to order a stay _____ proceedings. This means that the proceedings are stopped for a period of time.

9. In civil litigation, either a solicitor or a barrister may represent their client in court if they have rights of audience. If a solicitor wishes to use a barrister, they will draft a document called instructions _____ counsel. This document states what the solicitor is asking the barrister to do in the case.

10. After the defendant has served the defence on the claimant, the claimant

has the right to reply _____ the defence. They have a limited period of time in which to do this.

11. The judge reserved judgment in the case. When he returned to court he found _____ favour of the claimant and awarded damages of £34,000.

12. Each statement of case that a party wishes to issue at court and serve on the other parties must contain a statement _____ truth.

13. The judge explained to the claimant that they must prove that the defendant is liable on the balance _____ probabilities.

14. An attachment _____ earnings order is when the court decide that the defendant must pay the debt in instalments every month from their salary to the claimant.

15. The court can order that any interest _____ the damages must also be paid by the defendant to the claimant.

16. The court found that the defendant was liable _____ breach of contract.

17. The most common civil litigation claim is an action in the tort _____ negligence.

18. The claimant thought that the goods were defective and so brought an action _____ product liability.

19. Battery and assault are type of trespass __ the person.

20. I recently advised my client on a case about his neighbour trespassing ____ his property.

COLLOCATION GAP FILL

Complete the sentences using the correct collocation (answers are at the back of the book):

1. The newspaper reported that an allegation has been _____ against a local factory for nuisance. The claimant says that there is pollution coming from the factory and it is damaging the local environment.

2. An important principle of negligence is that any breach of a duty of care must _____ loss. There must be this connection between the breach and the loss.

3. If a potential defendant does not respond to a letter before action, the claimant may have no choice but to _____ a claim at their local county court.

4. In legal English the phrase to _____ to the court means to state an opinion to the court.

5. The legal English term that means to argue your case is to _____ your case to the court.

6. If a defendant states that they are not liable in any way, they _____ the allegations.

7. After a claimant has issued a claim against a defendant, the defendant has a limited period of time to _____ to the claim.

8. The court will expect all parties to attend the final hearing. The court may _____ against a party if they are not at court.

9. The English legal system is designed to produce settlements in cases. It is common for either party to _____ a Part 36 offer during the proceedings in order to settle the claim.

10. It is usual for a solicitor to brief a barrister before a _____

or a trial to make sure they are up to date with all developments in the case.

11. When a defendant or the defendant's advocate asks questions to the defendant about the case in court, the legal term is _____-____-_____.

12. After the court has heard all the evidence, the judge will _____ judgment.

13. If the losing party feels that the judgment of the court is incorrect, they can ask the court to _____ them _____ to appeal.

14. After the judge has read the judgment to the court, they will _____ an order. This means that they will officially state what the losing party has to do (for example, pay damages to the claimant, pay costs, comply with an injunction, etc).

15. One remedy for a claimant is to ask the court to _____ a contract. This means that the court will put the parties back in the position they were in, if the contract had never existed.

16. My neighbour always parks his car on my property. I will go to court and seek an _____ for him to stop.

17. It's so unfair that I had to pay for expensive lawyers to get my money from the defendant. I will _____ an order for costs from the court so he has to pay my legal fees.

18. The company lost a lot of money last year and so they _____ bankrupt after making an application to the court.

19. Some defendants do not pay their judgment debts on time, accordingly, bailiffs are sometimes employed by the court to _____ these judgments.

20. During proceedings, the court will _____ directions to the parties so that they know what they have to do and when to do it.

REPLACE THE INCORRECT WORD

Find and replace the *incorrect* word with the correct one (answers are at the back of the book):

1. The rules that govern civil litigation in England and Wales are known as the *Common* [_____] Procedure Rules.

2. If a defendant fails to file a defence or an acknowledgment of service on time, then the claimant can apply to the court for a *summary* [_____] judgment.

3. Both parties can attempt to resolve their dispute away from the court by organising Alternative *Disagreement* [_____] Resolution.

4. The person who repossesses property to pay for a judgment debt is known as a *Recorder* [_____].

5. If there are many claimants and/or many defendants in the same case, the court may order that the claims are heard together. This is known as a Group *Proceedings* [_____] Order.

6. The tort of interfering with another person's property or land is known as *nuisance* [_____].

7. The tort of stopping someone from quietly enjoying their own property or land is known as *trespass*. [_____].

8. If all the parties agree to settle the case, in legal English it is said that the matter has been *dissolved* [_____].

9. A defendant has three choices when they receive a claim form. They can *accept* [_____] the claim, deny the claim or file an acknowledgment of service.

10. The fastest and easiest route in the Civil Procedure Rules is called the small *claims* [_____] track. This is for low value, simple claims.

11. Usually a claim will have a claimant and a defendant. If there is another party to the proceedings who have an interest in the claim, they are called an *extra* [_____] party.

12. At the beginning of some hearings, the claimant and the defendant will be able to give an *initial* [_____] statement to the court, explaining their position in the case.

13. The judge may delay handing down their judgment to the parties. This gives them more time to consider their verdict. The legal English phrase used is to "*withhold* [_____] judgment".

14. It is possible for more than one person to be liable for a tort and for a group of people to be liable together. In this situation the phrase joint and *separate* [_____] liability can be used.

15. My friend James sold me a car last week. He said it was in good condition and didn't have any accidents. Later I discovered this was not true and so I am suing James for *negligence* [_____].

16. Another company copied my friend's book without her permission. She has issued proceedings against them for copyright *breach* [_____].

17. When a company does not have enough money to pay its creditors, specific proceedings called *bankruptcy* [_____ _____] proceedings can be brought against the company.

18. A witness *demand* [_____] is a court order that requires a witness to attend court or provide evidence.

19. The procedure for distributing the assets of a person who has just died is called *defamation* [_____]

20. If a defendant believes that a claim is brought that has little or no chance of success, they can make an application to the court for *default* [_____] judgment.

10 ANSWERS

True or False:

1. True

2. True

3. False

4. True

5. False

6. False

7. False

8. True

9. True

10. False

11. True

12. True

13. False

14. True

15. False

16. True

17. False

18. False

19. True

20. False

Vocabulary Gap Fill:

1. damages

2. allege

3. letter before action

4. overriding objective

5. claimant

6. brief

7. litigant in person

8. defend/deny

9. admit

10. applications

11. disclosure

12. multi-track

13. cross-examine

14. liable

15. verdict

16. award

17. mitigate

18. get divorced

19. breach

20. discrimination

Prepositions Gap Fill:

1. on

2. of

3. an

4. of

5. on

6. of

7. to

8. of

9. to

10. to

11. in

12. of

13. of

14. of

15. on

16. for

17. of

18. for

19. to

20. on

Collocations Gap Fill:

1. made

2. cause

3. issue

4. submit

5. plead

6. deny

7. respond

8. find

9. make

10. hearing

11. examination-in-chief

12. give

13. grant/leave

14. make

15. rescind

16. injunction

17. seek

18. went

19. enforce

20. give

Replace the Incorrect Word

1. ~~Common~~, Civil

2. ~~summary~~, default

3. ~~Disagreement~~, Dispute

4. ~~Recorder~~, Bailiff

5. ~~Proceedings~~, Litigation

6. ~~nuisance~~, trespass

7. ~~trespass~~, nuisance

8. ~~dissolved~~, resolved

9. ~~accept~~, admit

10. ~~Track~~, Court

11. ~~Extra~~, Third

12. ~~initial~~, opening

13. ~~withhold~~, reserve

14. ~~separate~~, several

15. ~~negligence~~, misrepresentation

16. ~~breach~~, infringement

17. ~~bankruptcy~~, insolvency

18. ~~demand~~, summons

19. ~~defamation~~, wills and probate

20. ~~default~~, summary

Legal Letter Writing

1. Language and Grammar Tips

Have a look at this real-life example of a legal opinion:

"The appellant complains that the trial court erred in holding that an attorney at law representing a loan association in the distribution of the proceeds of a loan to be made by such association could refuse to answer questions concerning such distribution on the ground that to answer would disclose a confidential communication to his client; and that the trial court erred in holding that a garnishee ordered by the court to appear for examination as to his indebtedness to the judgment debtor was the witness of the judgment creditor and could not be called for cross-examination by the latter."

Let's look at this by asking some questions about the above text.

1. What would you think if you received this from your lawyer?
2. How much of the text do you actually understand?
3. Why do you think this a bad example of legal writing?
4. How could it be improved?

4. Re-draft this sentence:

"I am herewith returning the contract with appropriate amendments, the same having been duly executed by me."

. . . .

. . . .

. . . .

What is good legal writing practice?

- **Know your audience** – Imagine you are the reader. Would you understand the letter/email? Why are you writing? What response do you want?

- **Front-load your document** – The reader's concentration will be at its highest at the start of the letter/email. Bring the important issue to the reader's attention in the subject line and the first sentence. Tell the reader why you are writing to them.

- **Context before detail** – Remind the reader of anything important that they may need to know to help their understanding of your letter/email (i.e. maybe the letter/email is replying to their letter/email).

- **State facts in simple form** – Keep the facts simple and to the point.

- **Avoid re-telling the story** — The reader will probably already have some knowledge of what you are writing about. You do not always need to repeat information, dates, etc.

- **Headings help** — Always use headings for longer letters and emails. Make sure the headings are in a logical order.

- **Write short paragraphs** – Long paragraphs will lose the reader's concentration and can easily lead to confusion.

- **Order is important**—A tidy, well-structured letter is more likely to make sense and be understood. Make sure your letter/email has a beginning, middle and end.

- **Check your document carefully** - Check, check and check again. Ask your superior if there is anything you think is incorrect or should not be included.

- **Keep it short** — If your letter/email is too long, there is a danger that your reader will not read all of it.

- **Do not "talk" in footnotes** – Do not use long footnotes in letters, although they are useful for citations.

- **Write short sentences** — As a rule, you should not include more than 18-20 words in a sentence. If it is longer, look for a logical break in the sentence and make it into two sentences.

- **Use active voice**—Passive voice is occasionally necessary, but try to avoid it.

- **Do Not begin sentences with "But" or "And".**

- **One word is usually enough** – Do not over complicate your letter/email. Can you use one word rather than two or three?

- **Do not use too much legalese** – it may sound strange, but it makes perfect sense. If you are writing to a client, they are probably not lawyers. There is no reason for them to understand legalese. Write your letter/email in plain English, with as little legalese as possible.

- **People have names** – Use names, not labels.

- **Use quotations but only if necessary** – Try to avoid using quotations unless they are fundamental to your point.

- **End on a helpful note** - Always leave yourself open to questions or queries about the letter/email. Invite the reader to contact you and provide your contact details at the end of the letter/email.

- **Enclose v Attach** – With letters you 'enclose' documents. With emails you 'attach' them.

Top Tips !

1. Passive v Active Voice

TIP: Use active voice where possible.

Examples,

Passive: 1) the finding was made by the court; 2) the particulars of claim was filed by the claimant; 3) It was held by the court that.

Active: 1) the court found; b) the claimant filed the particulars of claim; c) the court held that.

It is occasionally acceptable to use the passive voice, for instance when you do not know the person in the sentence or when the result is more important than the person.

2. Unnecessary verbs

TIP: Use one verb to describe one action.

Examples,

Unnecessary verbs: 1) reached a decision; 2) gave a ruling; 3) took action.

Plain English: 1) decided; 2) ruled; 3) acted.

3.   Use Names Not Labels

TIP: If you know the name of someone or something, then use it in legal writing.

Examples,

Labels: 1) The claimant; 2) The defendant; 3) The day in question.

Names (if known): 1) John Dean; 2) Molly Smythe; 3) 28th August 2014.

4.   Use Short Sentences

TIP Use full stops to break up long complicated sentences

Example,

"The court in Notting v. Jones, a case involving a similar building site accident, held that a person visiting the building site must adhere to the same standards as a person working on the building site, although it limited its holding to the facts of that case, which included the fact that the worker suffered from a disability."

"Notting v. Jones involved a similar building site accident. The court held that a visitor must adhere to the same standards as a person working on the building site. The ruling is limited to situations in which the worker suffers from a disability."

5.   Do not use three words when only one is necessary

TIP: Try to avoid using exhaustive lists. Letters and emails are not contracts and so do not need to be drafted in the same style. Unless it is important to list similar things, try to use one general word or, sometimes, just the first word of the list.

Examples,

Lists: 1) "Every house, flat, or office in the street"; 2) "wine, beer and spirits"; 3) "Give, devise and bequeath".

Simple words: 1) "Every building"; 2) "alcohol"; 3) "Give".

6. Meaningless adjectives and adverbs

TIP: Do not use unnecessary adjectives and adverbs to try to make your point stronger. It can have the opposite effect.

Example,

Meaningless Adjectives and Adverbs: "Your client clearly, carelessly and negligently caused the accident. It is our position that our client was blatantly not at fault. We have no other feasible option but to respectfully file a claim with the court forthwith."

Plain legal English: "Your client caused the accident. Our client is not at fault. We have no option but to file a claim with the court."

7. Double Negatives

TIP: Avoid double negatives. They are likely to cause confusion.

Examples,

Double Negatives: not uncommon, failed to show non-compliance, not insignificant, not uncomplicated, no small, not incapable, not inappropriate.

Plain legal English: common, showed ability, significant, complicated, large part, capable, ...

8.   Unnecessary Archiac and Meaningless Phrases

TIP: If you think your recipient will not understand the full sentence, change it and make it simpler. Do not use old traditional legal words if plain English can be used in its place. Also, try to avoid meaningless opening statements. They add nothing of substance. Concentrate on the important aspects of your letter/email rather than flowery unnecessary words and phrases.

Examples,

Old legalese: Hereby, Herewith, Hereupon, Forthwith, Notwithstanding, Therein, Thereby Thereupon, Nonetheless

Meaningless Opening statements: I would like to point out, It should be noted that, Despite the fact, In fact, It is obvious, It is clear.

2. Salutations and Sign-offs

Recipient	Salutation	Sign-Off
Unknown name and gender	Dear Sir or Madam,	Yours faithfully
Unknown man	Dear Sir,	Yours faithfully
Unknown woman	Dear Madam,	Yours faithfully
Known married or single man	Dear Mr *"Surname"*. For example, Dear Mr Jones,	Yours sincerely
Known married woman	Dear Mrs *"Surname"*. For example, Dear Mrs Jones,	Yours sincerely
Known single woman	Dear Miss *"Surname"*. For example, Dear Miss Jones,	Yours sincerely
Known woman, unknown marital status	Dear Ms *"Surname"*. For example, Dear Ms Jones,	Yours sincerely
Unknown couple	Dear Sir and Madam,	Yours faithfully
Known married couple	Dear Mr and Mrs Jones,	Yours sincerely
Known unmarried couple	Dear Mr Jones and Ms Robinson,	Yours sincerely

Known person and specific title	Dear Dr Jones, Dear Professor Jones, Dear Judge Jones,	Yours sincerely
Colleague	Dear *"Full First Name"*. For example, Dear Jonathan,	Yours sincerely

3. Opening Sentences

Starting the chain of dialogue.

By way of introduction, I am writing to you on behalf of my client XYZ ltd in relation to the contract with your client, ZYX ltd dated 21 May.

We are writing to you on behalf of our client, XYZ ltd in relation to the lease of 22 Blackthorne Close, North Malling.

We are instructed by XYZ ltd in the matter of the boundary dispute with your client.

Replying to correspondence

We are writing to confirm safe receipt of your letter and attachments dated 12 July.

I refer to your letter dated 12 July.

Thank you for your letter dated 12 July.

We write with reference to our telephone conversation earlier today.

Specific openings

I trust you are well. I am writing with an update on your claim against XYZ ltd.

I apologise for the delay in replying to your letter of 12 July.

I am pleased to inform you that the local authority has approved your planning application.

I regret to inform you that the court has not granted a time extension to file your witness statement.

Making requests

We write in relation to your client ZYX ltd. We would be grateful if you could seek your client's instructions on the latest draft of the shipping contract sent on 12 July.

Many thanks for the instructions on the proposed claim against ZYX ltd. Please could you be so kind as to confirm in writing that you wish to go ahead and issue the claim.

4. Closing Sentences

Standard Closing Sentences

I look forward to hearing from you.

Please do not hesitate to contact me if you have any questions.

I understand that you may wish to discuss this in person or on the telephone, so please do contact me and we can arrange a meeting.

We will take instructions from our client and will contact you in due course.

We would be grateful if you could seek your client's instructions as soon as possible.

Enclosing or Attaching Documents

I enclose/attach* ....

Please find enclosed/attached* ....

I would be grateful if you could sign and date the enclosed contract and send it back to me.

I would be grateful if you could print off and sign the contract attached to this email and return it to me as soon as possible.

* Remember to use enclose with paper letters and attach with emails and faxes.

5. Letter Writing Exercises and Examples

Legal Writing: Task 1 – Short email to client

You are an associate at a large law firm, Whitethornes & Co. You have received the following email from your supervising partner, Judy Smith, requesting that you get in touch with a client to seek instructions on a matter. Your task is to draft a simple email to the client passing on Judy's requests in her email below.

From	Judy Smith
To	You
Date	11 March 2015
Subject	Task1 Corp: Instructions
Hi,	

Hi,

I have something urgent for you to do. Please could you get in touch with Sally Williams at Task1 Corp and seek further instructions. The other side are asking for our comments on the shipping contract with their client, We Ship Everything Ltd. I need her comments on the pricing structure, notice period and return policy for the goods. We need her instructions so we can amend the contract. Also, please ask when they are free for a conference call on this. I need the comments by close of business tomorrow so maybe the call can be set up for this afternoon.

Finally, I spoke to Clive Walker from the litigation department. He has read the papers now. Please ask Sally to call him.

Please cc me in on all correspondence.

Thanks

Judy

Example Answer for Task 1

Dear Sally,

I have been asked by my supervising partner Judy Smith to request further instructions from you in relation to the shipping contract with We Ship Everything Ltd.

Specifically, we require your comments on the pricing structure, notice period and return policy for the goods. Please could you check your calendar and let me know if you are free for a conference call later this afternoon. We are free at 3pm. Judy has requested that we have your comments by the end of tomorrow. We can then amend the contract and send it to the other side.

Finally, Judy has spoken to Clive Walker from our litigation department. He has reviewed the paperwork you sent him. Please could you call him to discuss. His number is 123,4567,8901.

I have cc'd Judy in on this email.

Please do not hesitate to contact me if you have any questions.

Kind regards

. . . .

Legal Writing: Task 2 – Long email to colleague

Following on from the conference call with your supervising partner Judy Smith and Sally Williams from Task1 Corp, you have been asked to provide some legal research on certain parts of the contract. Sally wants to know what provisions could be included in the contract to reduce the risk of non-payment of invoices. Your notes on the research are below. Judy has approved your research and has asked you to email Sally. Draft an email advising Sally of her options.

Notes for Judy Re: Task1 Corp

What payment options are suitable and how can we reduce the chances of non-payment?

Option 1 - Have an agreed payment period (say 30 days in which to receive payment in full)· Problem is how to enforce? Letter to request payment, Open dialogue with debtor· If no payment, letter before action· If still no payment, no choice but to issue proceedings for full amount plus costs· This is not ideal as the risk is with Task1 Corp·

Option 2 - Ask for full money before delivery of goods· This is better than option 1, but not every customer will be in a financial position to do this (maybe cash flow problems)· Plus it is far riskier for the customer and so Task1 Corp may receive fewer orders and receive less income.

Option 3 - Ask for a deposit (20%) plus a guarantee. This is standard market practice for goods of this type and value. Possibly a good compromise. Sally wants the contract signed quickly so maybe this is the best option.

Example Answer for Task 2

Subject: Research on payment provisions in sale of goods contract

Dear Judy,

[Beginning - Introducing the reason for the email]

Further to our conference call yesterday, I have had a chance to research the issues discussed in relation to your options in case of non-payment of invoices.

Specifically, you asked me to provide you with the most common legal options for a seller to include in a sale of goods contract to deal with non-payment of an invoice.

[Middle – Setting out your research in full]

The first option is to include a payment period so that both parties can plan their cash flow. This also gives the buyer a chance to inspect the goods before they pay for them. This option is not ideal for Task1 Corp as you will be at risk of non-payment and you would then have to enforce payment after they have received the goods. This can be done informally at first through phone calls and letters before action. The ultimate option here would be to issue proceedings at court to obtain payment.

The second option is to request payment in full before you deliver the goods to the buyer. This is less risky as you will be paid before you send the goods to the customer. However, the commercial implications may mean that you will receive fewer orders. Customers may not have sufficient funds to make the payment. These customers may buy from another seller who do not insist on full payment.

The third option is to request a deposit, for example, 20%. This is common for your market and type of product. You are at less risk as you receive a proportion of the payment before you deliver the goods. You could then insist on a payment period for the rest of the payment. This appears to be market practice and a suitable compromise. I would advise this option.

[End – Asking for further instructions and informing the client what happens next. Plus contact details]

Please let me know what you would like to do with regards to the contract. I will then go ahead and draft the provisions in the contract.

If you wish to discuss any of the above, please contact me on 0207 123 4567.

Kind regards

. . . .

Legal Writing: Task 3: Formal letter to court enclosing documents

Clive Walker, a partner from the litigation department has spoken to Sally about a different legal matter. Proceedings have been issued against a customer who has not paid their invoices. The deadline for filing witness statements is tomorrow. Sally is having problems collating information for her to make her witness statement. Clive has suggested that she makes an application to the court to extend the time limit for this witness statement to be filed with the court. He has also advised the court that he will be unable to attend the Case Management Conference on 25th August. He would like to ask the court to re-schedule for a week later. Clive has given you the following information:

- Your law firm's address: The Old Building, 120 Norwich Street, North Town, NM3 4RT
- The court's address: North Town County Court, High Street, North Town, NM1 3GH
- Parties to the claim: Task1 Corp v Holbron Shipping Ltd
- The claim number: NM100 AA 342
- The application form for the time extension
- Court fee of £50

He has asked you to draft a letter enclosing the relevant documents and requesting that the court grant the time extension.

Write a letter to the court following Clive's instructions.

Example answer for Task 3

The Old Building

120 Norwich Street

North Town

NM3 4RT

11 March 2015

North Town County Court

High Street

North Town

NM1 3GH

Dear Sir or Madam,

In the matter of Task1 Corp v Holbron Shipping Ltd

Claim Number: NM100 AA 342

We act for the claimant in the above matter. The parties are currently preparing witness statements as scheduled by the Case Management Conference. The deadline for filing the witness statements is tomorrow.

Unfortunately, our client has been unable to collate all relevant documentation needed to prepare their witness statement. We understand that they require another week in which to complete the statement with exhibits.

Accordingly, please find enclosed an application with the court fee to request a one-week time extension for the filing of the witness statement and exhibits. We have also written to the defendant's solicitors requesting their agreement. We would be grateful for the court's agreement to this time extension.

Finally, we also request that the next Case Management Conference be re-scheduled from 25th August to 2nd September. Instructing solicitors are unable to attend on the 25th August. We have also requested agreement from the defendant's solicitors to this re-scheduling.

We would be grateful if the court would agree to both requests in writing.

Please do not hesitate to contact us on 0207 123 4567 if you have any questions.

Yours faithfully,

Whitethornes & Co

Legal Writing: Task 4: Formal letter to other side's solicitors enclosing documents

Clive Walker has also requested that you draft a letter to the other side's solicitors to explain the application to the court to extend the time limit for the witness statement. He also wants to ask them if they will agree to re-schedule the Case Management Conference on 25th August to a week later. Clive has given you the following information:

- Your law firm's address: The Old Building, 120 Norwich Street, North Town, NM3 4RT.
- The other side's solicitors: Rowan Brown & Co, 80 Long Street, South Town, NM3 8YU
- Our client: Task1 Corp
- Their client: Holbron Shipping Ltd
- Our reference: CP 345/1
- Their reference: RB 2221/1a
- Application for time extension

He has asked you to draft a letter enclosing the relevant documents and requesting that the other side agree to the time extension.

Draft a letter to the other side following Clive's instructions.

Example answer to Task 4

The Old Building

120 Norwich Street

North Town

NM3 4RT

11 March 2015

Our reference: CP 345/1

Rowan Brown & Co

80 Long Street

South Town

NM3 8YU

Dear Sir or Madam,

Your client: Holbron Shipping Ltd

Your reference: RB 2221/1a

We write in relation to the matter Task Corp v Holbron Shipping Ltd.

As you are aware, the time limit for filing witness statements in the above matter is tomorrow. Our client informs us that they are unable to collate all relevant documentation and will not be in a position to file their witness statement on time. We are writing to request a short time extension to file the witness statement of one week. Please could you confirm your agreement to this short extension in writing by email today. We have made an application to the court to request a one-week extension and we enclose this for your information.

Also, we are unable to attend the Case Management Conference scheduled for 25th August. Please could you agree to re-schedule this conference to 2nd September. Again, we would be grateful if you could confirm this agreement in writing.

Please do not hesitate to contact us on 0207 123 4567 if you have any questions.

Yours faithfully,

Whitethornes & Co

Legal Writing Task 5: Memo to a colleague requesting legal research

Your supervising partner Judy Smith has come back with more information from Task Corp and their contract negotiations with We Ship Everything Ltd. She wants you to look into a contract law point for her and to check some case law on creating a binding contract. Specifically, the client wants a summary in relation to contracts for shipping goods and the law in relation to any specific legal obligations of offer, acceptance and consideration for contacts for shipping goods from China to the UK. She wants cases and any relevant legislation.

As you are going on holiday next week, Judy agrees that you can delegate this piece of research to a colleague. Judy needs the research by the end of next week.

Draft a memo to a colleague asking them to conduct this piece of research for Judy.

Example answer to Task 5

From	You
To	Daniel Ameobi
Date	11 March 2015
Subject	Task1 Corp: Legal Research

Hi Daniel,

I wonder if you can help me. I work for Judy Smith in the commercial department and she has asked me to conduct some research for her. I am away on holiday next week, so she has asked if you are able to do this for her instead while I am away.

The background of the research is this: we act for Task1 Corp who ship goods to and from many countries around the world. Recently, they want to ship from China to the UK but they want to know the law in relation to the creation of legally binding contracts between these two jurisdictions. Could you please look into the relevant case law and legislation for the legal obligations required for the creation of contracts between China and the UK. Specifically, Judy would like to know the law in relation to making an offer, acceptance and consideration for creating shipping contracts for these two jurisdictions.

Judy would like the research by the end of next week.

I am on holiday next week, so please come and talk to me today (or before I leave for my holiday) if you need anything. My phone extension is 6746. Please call if you have any questions.

Thanks very much for your assistance.

. . . .

ABOUT THE AUTHOR

Michael Howard is a solicitor and legal English lecturer from London. After many years of legal practice he decided to travel around Europe and the Middle East lecturing law and teaching legal English. His travels took him to Poland, Germany, Dubai, Abu Dhabi and finally back to the UK where he was invited to teach legal English to foreign lawyers and law students at courses run at Cambridge University. Michael now works in legal publishing and spends his free time writing legal English courses, dictionaries and exercise books to help foreign lawyers improve their legal English.

Legal Disclaimer: This book contains information on legal vocabulary. It is written for the benefit of lawyers, law students and business professionals whose first language is not English. The information is not advice and should not be treated as such. You must not rely on the information in the book as legal, financial, taxation, or accountancy advice. If you have any specific questions about any legal, financial, or accountancy matters you should consult an appropriately qualified professional. We do not represent, warrant, undertake or guarantee that the information in the book is correct, accurate, complete or non-misleading or that the use of the language in this book will lead to any particular outcome or result.

Made in the USA
Middletown, DE
04 February 2023